TO TELL OUR STORIES

Holocaust Survivors of Southern Arizona

To Tell Our Stories

Holocaust Survivors of Southern Arizona

Presented by:

Jewish Family and Children's Services of Southern Arizona

Contents

* of blessed memory at the time of publication

* of blessed memory at the time of publication

This book is dedicated to Holocaust Survivors
who made Southern Arizona their home

and

to the six million Jews
and the millions of other innocents
unable to tell us their stories

Introduction

Raisa Moroz and Richard Fenwick believe passionately that we must never forget. This collection of stories, written by Survivors in Southern Arizona, is possible because of that shared commitment, respect and friendship, and their unique combination of expertise and life experience.

The Moroz family immigrated to the United States from Belarus in 1996 because of rampant anti-Semitism in what was then the Soviet Union. Raisa, her husband Valeriy, their two daughters, and her in-laws were aided by HIAS, an organization that rescues people whose lives are in danger for being who they are. Raisa's parents and other family members joined them later. Along with hundreds of others from many countries, the family became U.S. citizens in 2001.

Jewish Family and Children's Services of Southern Arizona helped the Moroz family make this challenging transition. They were resettled by the agency, and Raisa was hired by JFCS for her first job in the U.S. She then joined the Jewish Federation of Southern Arizona staff for almost 12 years. She returned to JFCS in 2009 as a Case Manager for the Holocaust Survivor Program and became the Program Manager a few months later.

Raisa began asking her Russian-speaking clients to pen stories about their lives. She created a list of questions and they began writing. Raisa quickly realized that their stories would not be widely appreciated because of language barriers.

As luck would have it, Richard, a retired USAF Russian linguist, volunteered to partner with Raisa in 2010 to curate a collection of stories from Holocaust Survivors in Southern Arizona. He translated those written in Russian, transcribed verbally recorded stories as the project expanded, and reviewed stories written in English by Survivors from other European countries. You will discover these autobiographical stories in this remarkable book.

Richard, a parent and grandparent as well, worked in the defense industry for six years after his Air Force retirement in 2000. He is a musician, writer and poet, and after leaving private industry he gave himself a few years to write, which resulted in a published book of poetry and another on the way. During that time, he also cared for his beloved mother and father.

He discovered JFCS, was introduced to Raisa, and her story project became their project, flourishing in the process. Richard also visits weekly with Russian-speaking Survivors, helps them with day-to-day translation needs, and provides logistics for group events. He loves the "work" and quickly developed great affection for the Survivors and agency staff he has befriended.

Their volunteer partnership continues with an open invitation to other Survivors in Southern Arizona to tell their stories. They look forward to a second edition of this book.

Fred Fruchthendler   Carlos A. Hernández MA, LCSW, CPHQ
Chair, Board of Directors   President & CEO
JFCS of Southern Arizona   JFCS of Southern Arizona

The Holocaust is often defined in sets of numbers. We read, for example, that six million Jews were killed as the Nazis brutally and methodically carried out "the final solution" across Europe. Reading further, we learn that this number represented fully two-thirds of the entire European Jewish population at that time. Yet numbers like this can become staggering, almost too difficult to wrap our minds around.

We agree that the numbers, the statistics, must be remembered. At the same time, we're certain that a proper education of the Holocaust can only be gained when we combine numbers with the personal accounts of those who survived. The statistics remain in rote memory; but the personal accounts are what make the terror of the Holocaust very real in our minds. It is worth insisting we pay attention to these accounts.

We began this project in 2010 as a way to introduce readers to the Holocaust as it transpired in the Soviet Union. The Nazis moved so swiftly across Belarus and Ukraine – Soviet Republics – that there was little time to establish a streamlined way to deport Soviet Jews to camps west of there. Undeterred, the Nazis found new ways to maintain their mandate: Jews unable to evacuate deeper into the Soviet Union were executed by firing squad, or rounded up to be burned in barns. At Babi Yar, a ravine in Kiev, the Nazis and local sympathizers executed nearly 34,000 Jews in just two days. In Belarus, 90 percent of the Jewish prewar population was destroyed. Another statistic – but one you should keep in mind when reading those accounts written here by Belorussian Jews living now in Southern Arizona.

As the project expanded, we determined to include the personal accounts of other European Jews as well. Most of us are better informed as to what occurred in the Polish extermination camps, and how Jews from a wide swath of Europe were transported, selected, and summarily murdered upon their arrival at a camp. For this reason, these particular accounts will seem more familiar to you. You'll also learn about less-organized concentration camps established in the Soviet Union, places such as Akhmetchetka and Domanevka in Ukraine.

We ask that you keep one important fact in mind as you read these histories: if you are a Southern Arizonan, these survivors are your honored neighbors. Some stories here are simpler than others, and some are more plainly written; all are the memories of childhood or teenage years. And all will touch your heart in various ways.

For example, David will tell you how his grandparents were tossed into a well and left to die; Boris will explain his mother's dilemma when forced to choose which child she'd save; Valeria will describe being a twin and a test subject in a death camp; and Walter will show you the ingenuity it took for a teenager to survive a labor camp.

We are not experts on the Holocaust; our normal function is to provide support to survivors in Southern Arizona as much as possible. However, as this project took root, we gained a tremendous amount of information related to the cold precision the Nazis used in implementing the destruction of millions of families.

70 years have passed since World War II ended. We are fortunate and grateful to have this last generation of survivors in our midst to provide us the gift of their stories. We are convinced that every Holocaust survivor's personal account represents one piece of a vast puzzle, and we thank those survivors who agreed to share their stories. We are, all of us, obliged to educate ourselves and our children, in any way we can, to the dangers of thinking less of another human based simply on belief and prejudice.

Raisa Moroz
Holocaust Program Manager
JFCS of Southern Arizona

Richard Fenwick
Holocaust Program Volunteer
JFCS of Southern Arizona

TO TELL OUR STORIES

Holocaust Survivors of Southern Arizona

Liliya Beskina

I was born in 1929 in Rostov-on-Don, Russia. My father was a therapist and my mother was a housewife. On my father's side I had three uncles and four aunts, while on my mother's side I had three uncles and two aunts. I was twelve years old when the war began, and had just finished the fifth grade. We were at Pioneer camp on the Sea of Azov when we heard the news about the war, and returned immediately to Rostov-on-Don after that.[1]

My father was drafted into the Army three days later and was sent to the front with four of my uncles. Four months later, as the Germans approached Rostov, we evacuated in railroad freight cars. The Germans bombed our train repeatedly as we traveled, but we finally made it to Makhachkala, where I finished the sixth grade.[2] I would go to the hospital there to care for the wounded, along with other students. We fed them and wrote letters home for them. We helped in any way we could.

The German offensive in the north Caucuses continued into the summer of 1942. Once they were close to Makhachkala we evacuated again. This time we went to Alma-Ata, in central Asia.[3] I finished the seventh grade there, in 1943. We were constantly hungry, even though my mother worked at home sewing belts made of leftover leather strips. I helped her make these belts.

Other than one letter, sent in July 1941, we hadn't heard from my father for two years. Then later that summer a relative in Moscow read an article in *Ogonyok* about German brutalities that had occurred in the

---

[1] The Young Pioneers was a Soviet youth organization for children aged 10–15.
[2] Makhachkala is in the Republic of Dagestan, Russia.
[3] Alma-Ata, now called Almaty, is the largest city in Kazakhstan.

prison camp at Khorol, Ukraine.[4] My father was mentioned in the article, which included his picture. This is how we learned he was alive. The Germans had taken him prisoner during the battle for Kiev and sent him to Khorol, where he was routinely tortured. He escaped the camp with the help of locals, who hid him in a potato pit for nearly three months until they could get him to a partisan unit.

When Khorol was liberated, in 1943, my father helped restore the city before leaving with the army. By the time the war ended, he'd gone as far as Prague, Czechoslovakia. Besides *Ogonyok*, his time in Khorol prison camp was detailed in a Red Army magazine. He was demobilized from the Army in 1946.

My father was haunted for the rest of his life with memories of the camp. He worked as a family doctor, but was arrested in January 1953 when the purge of Jewish doctors began.[5] Several months after Stalin died he was rehabilitated and freed from prison.

The Germans also imprisoned my father's brother, Semyon Veksler, in Kiev. He was a nearby village doctor. We only learned in 2002 that the Germans executed him along with the seriously wounded.

We returned to Rostov-on-Don following its liberation in 1944, and the war ended on May 9, 1945. Two years later I started at the medical institute, where I completed my studies in 1953. I worked five years in pediatrics, then 30 years with tuberculosis patients, first children and then adults.

I was reminded I was Jewish my whole life. Children in school teased me, and after I graduated from the medical institute I couldn't find work right away for the same reason. I'd been promised a position in a children's hospital after the hospital I worked in was converted for adults in 1975, but the senior doctor at the children's clinic personally told me he wouldn't give the job to a Jew. I had to stay at the adult tuberculosis clinic.[6]

---

[4] *Ogonyok*, first published in 1899, is one of the oldest magazines in Russia.

[5] In 1952 a group of prominent Moscow doctors, primarily Jewish, was accused of conspiring to kill Soviet leaders. This "Doctor's Plot" led to the dismissal or arrest of numerous doctors nationwide. Krushchev denounced the conspiracy in 1955.

[6] Liliya Beskina immigrated to the US in 2000. She passed away April 24, 2012.

Michael Bokor

Hungary

I was born in Budapest, Hungary, where I lived until the war ended in January 1945. There'd been growing anti-Semitism over the years in Hungary, and we were very restricted – even though I was a child – as to what we could and couldn't do. I went to school there for eight years. The eighth grade was the most difficult because that was when we started wearing the stars. I managed to get through it because my parents were with me, although my father was mostly being used in forced labor. He came home every now and then, but my mother had to take care of me and my two sisters alone.

Things started getting really bad in about April 1943, when the Nazis took power in Hungary. That's when Jews were enemy number one. We were persecuted and couldn't go to school, so after eight years of school I tried to get a job as an apprentice. When the Germans finally occupied Budapest, all hell broke loose.

The Hungarian Nazis were worse than the Germans. We spent the end of 1943 into 1944 mostly in hiding, moving from one building to another to try to save ourselves. Our building had a big yellow star on it, and we weren't allowed to leave during curfew. But a friend and I decided to go to a Swedish-owned house near the Danube River. Sweden was a neutral country which made this house a safe place to go. When it was still foggy early one morning, we took our stars off and left our apartments to get to that Swedish house. But once we got there they told us to come back with our families, so we returned home to do that.

I wish I'd had my family with me when I'd first gone, because near our building a Nazi SS soldier caught us and asked us to identify ourselves. Naturally we couldn't, so he examined us. He had his bayonet against my back, but my friend took off running. He ran as fast as he could into our building, while the soldier stayed with me. The soldier yelled that if he didn't come out they would take everyone in the building away.

He took us to German headquarters, not far from where we lived. An SS guard made us go upstairs, where another German officer lectured us as to what we weren't allowed to do. He told another guard to take us to the Hungarian Nazi headquarters, known as the "Arrow Cross" in English.[1] My friend was one year older than me and was taken downstairs, where people went and never returned. I was told to go upstairs, to an empty room, where a man came in and beat me severely. My mouth and nose were bleeding and my teeth hurt. I was fifteen years old and crying. He left without saying a word. Then a tall blond man came in who said to me, "Why are you here?" I told him I had broken curfew, and he told me to leave and to tell the people at the gate that it had been a mistake, which I did. Then I ran home.

20 years later I was working in Los Angeles and met a Hungarian Jew who knew that blond man's name. It turns out he was Jewish and had infiltrated the Nazi operation. Someone must have been watching over me, because I got out of that building. It was a miracle. Once you got caught like that there was no such thing as making it home.

About a week later they took my mother to a concentration camp. They raided our building and said that anyone over 15 had to go. At first it was 25 to 30 people, but every day after they'd take more. Within four or five weeks everybody had to go: men, women, and children. My friend and I went into hiding, and my mother was taken away. My sisters were twelve and eight years old, so at first they didn't have to go, though later they did. They'd been put into a ghetto in the central part of Budapest, closed off except for one gate and guarded by the Nazis. My sisters stayed with my father's sister, who was already there. They found a place in a basement, which was also used as a bomb shelter.

While my family was in the ghetto, my friend and I hid in the various bombed out apartment buildings in the city and took food from abandoned apartments. We were smart enough to think no one would search for us. We snuck from building to building at night and took food

---

[1] The Arrow Cross Party, Hungary's national socialist party, led the nation from October 1944 to March 1945. The party was ruthlessly anti-Semitic.

from pantries, but after about a month we ran out of places to go. I decided to go into the ghetto to be with my family.

People were dead or dying in the streets. I remember there was a pharmacy near us where a pile of dead bodies was stacked up like wood, yellow in color. People started burying their relatives in parks, but the graves were shallow and sometimes you could see a hand sticking out of the ground. That's what it was like to live in the ghetto: stepping over dead people and not being able to do anything about it.

Starvation and contaminated water plagued the ghetto, and people there died from lack of food or disease. We slept on dirty floors with just a few blankets and occasionally had small amounts of food, like tomato soup and barley. To this day I won't eat tomato soup. When someone died we'd go through their pockets, searching for food. Sometimes they had sugar cubes or cookies. We'd take whatever they had.

The Russians arrived on January 17, 1945, and broke through a wall in our basement. They entered the basement and went straight up the stairs to fight the Germans. They were actually Ukrainians, and they weren't very nice to us even though we were wearing stars. They just shoved us aside and kept going. But we were free.

The next day we were in the streets looting, which everyone did. For me, this was the end of the war. Many feared that the Germans would return, and many of the Hungarian army guys suddenly became "nice people." Some were hung from telephone and light poles, because there were Jews who took revenge. We found a lot of food in one house, so we took it and ate until we were sick.

My father, who'd been taken to a labor camp, had been a Hungarian soldier for years, but when these things started happening they converted him to use as forced labor. Around 1943 they took the uniforms away from the Jewish soldiers, who then had to wear yellow bands and work as laborers. Many of them died, and many were taken to Russia. That's where my uncle died. My father happened to be a carriage driver as well, so he drove Hungarian soldiers various places. He was aware of where we were and how we were doing, but he could do nothing when my mother was taken away. He tried to find us, but we were in the ghetto and he couldn't come in or out so we lost touch with him until after the war. My father and his entire labor group were put into a camp.

Both of my parents survived but came home separately. I was liberated in January 1945, but I didn't see my parents until around the end of May that year. My father came home first, followed shortly after that by my mother. The important thing is that we survived.

My grandparents died in concentration camps. My uncle and cousins from the villages all died in Auschwitz. The laborers were taken to the front lines without adequate clothing, and when winter came they froze to death. That was the story of the Hungarian solders.

We couldn't all come to America together because the authorities only allowed a certain number of people from each country to enter each year. The Hungarian quota was filled, but my mother was born in an area that had belonged to Slovakia, so we came to America with Czechoslovakian visas. My mother and I finally arrived in September 1947, but my father had to wait until November 1948, since he'd been born in the middle of Hungary. We spent two years prior to that in a Displaced Persons camp in Germany, a camp for refugees. We lived there in a huge stable partitioned off with wax paper for families.

There was no point in staying in Hungary. It was no better than before. Besides, the Russians were there, and they were ruthless. They'd picked up my father many times to go to their labor camps, but he kept escaping. I was picked up several times as well.

In America we lived in poverty in the worst part of downtown New York, but our rent was paid by a Jewish agency. I had some training in making handbags as an apprentice in Hungary, so we made purses to sell. These were hard times, but we made it to America, and though we didn't prosper over the years, we made it. I served in the intelligence field in the U.S. Army because I spoke several languages. After the Army I started over in California, where my parents came to live with me.

Vilyam Bukhman

Ukraine

My name is Vilyam Bukhman, born in 1926 in the town of Chechelnik in the Vinnitsa region of Ukraine. My mother, Dyshel Leybovna Sherstyanaya, was born in 1897 in Torgovets, several kilometers from the city of Uman. She was the eleventh child in the poor family of a miller, and the first Jewish girl to attend a Russian school. She also passed the exams to enter gymnasium in the seventh grade.[1] Her family was very poor, and some of the children moved to Brazil as adults. She taught at a Jewish School after the revolution, and after that she worked in an orphanage. She met my father in 1921.

My father, Aron Peysakh Leybovich Bukhman, was born in 1896 in Chechelnik. He had an older brother, Srul, and a younger sister, Sheyva. My father was shot by bandits during the civil war but survived.[2] He spent the rest of his life as an invalid paralyzed on his right side. We moved to Odessa in 1937, where he completed training courses to learn how to write with his left hand. He became a bookkeeper, which allowed him to provide for his family for the rest of his life.

My older brother Lev died in 1930. I had two other brothers: Israil, my middle brother, was born in 1932, and my younger brother Ilya was born in 1937. We lived in two small towns, Savran and Krivoye Ozero, until 1937 when we moved to Odessa. I finished the fourth grade in Krivoye Ozero, and in Odessa I was able to complete the eighth grade prior to the start of the war.

---

[1] A gymnasium was a secondary school comparable to college prep school.
[2] Russia's Civil War followed the 1917 Revolution and lasted into the early 1920s.

The Great Patriotic War began on June 22, 1941.[3] That day my friends and I heard aircraft and ran up a hill to see what was happening towards Odessa's military harbor. A Russian Navy destroyer was shooting at German aircraft, but the Germans bypassed the port and turned towards the city. Bombs fell very close to our house, and one of the neighboring buildings collapsed when it was hit. That's when we ran home.

Up to that time I'd read a lot about German atrocities during the war, and had heard radio broadcasts about how the fascists behaved as they occupied territories. Knowing this, I began asking my parents to leave Odessa. People were already evacuating by train, and many were leaving on ships. At one point we even loaded our things on a ship, but at the last minute my parents decided to go by train. This turned out to be the right choice, since we later found out that the ship had been sunk.

My mother's nephew, Fima Sherstyanoy, served in the Red Army and learned that trains were being organized to evacuate citizens. He came to us and other relatives and put us on the last train leaving the city.

The evacuation was extremely difficult. We traveled an entire week from Odessa to Nikolaev (a two-hour trip in normal conditions), and on the way we were repeatedly bombed.

The Germans bombed our train two days after we left Odessa. People on the train jumped from the boxcars and ran into nearby woods, which was also a complete swamp. The small children cried and hung onto the adults. I had to search for my family because everyone had scattered. Eventually the locomotive driver signaled us and everyone ran back to their boxcars.

The train continued on, and after a week we arrived at Varvarovka, the last stop before Nikolaev. This particular day is burned into my memory, as German airplanes flew out of the clouds and began bombing the station while we were there. Once again, everyone jumped out of the boxcars, this time running to a sandy embankment. My little brother, just four years old, ran with me. I was afraid for him and lay him down on the embankment, then covered his body with mine. We lie there motionless as the enemy fired. But apparently G-d wanted us to stay

---

[3] "Great Patriotic War" is the term most often used for World War II in the former Soviet Union. It is still in use today.

alive. When the attack ended, people who survived (including my brother Ilya and I) ran back to the boxcars and our train continued on. We left the dead on that sandy embankment, now red with their blood.

At Kherson we were bombed again, and again we ran and hid, though my brother cried and repeated: "Vilya, my legs hurt." I put him on my shoulders and ran.

They bombed us at Melitopol as well, and again we all scattered. It was nighttime, and I ended up with my Aunt Sheyba in a different car, one used for refrigeration. They locked us inside, where people were crying and children were screaming. There were more than 60 people in the refrigeration car, knocking and begging to be let out, going to the bathroom in the wagon. It was terrible. There was no way to breathe and many could have died. Passers-by heard strange sounds and couldn't understand where they were coming from. Luckily someone figured it out and opened the doors, and people began falling from the car. Aunt Sheyba and I spotted my mother, father, and brothers in the crowd that had gathered nearby, and we cried with joy that we were alive. My family thought they would never see us again.

My parents told us we would not be going any farther. After Melitopol the Germans stopped bombing the train, so we reached the relative calm of Mariupol, where my mother's sister and older brother Sender lived. He had five sons, all of them away in the war.

I was only fifteen years old, but I'd read in the papers and heard on the radio that German forces were on the move in the west and we needed to keep going. I understood that the Germans were advancing to the north, and in all probability would cut off Mariupol, which wasn't far from the Sea of Azov to the south. We would find ourselves in their trap. I told my father and mother that we would perish if we remained, insisting that we leave immediately. My parents listened to me, got the tickets, and we traveled to Gorky, to the north. My mother asked her sister and brother-in-law to come with us, but her sister's husband refused. He said the Germans were a cultured and civil people and wouldn't kill anyone, not even the Jews; he also said it was all propaganda designed to scare us. They decided to remain behind, and they perished.

We traveled for about eight days to the north and reached the transfer station at Kinel, from which the trains went south to Tashkent. We boarded a train going to Uzbekistan. We'd heard that the Germans had cut the rail lines leading to Mariupol, which they'd entered without resistance.

We reached Tashkent, stopped briefly at Andijan, and then arrived at the regional center of Grunch-Mazar, where we stayed. My Uncle Srul and his wife Anya (Khana) and their son Isya went on to the city of Osh.

We were given a room in Grunch-Mazar (about 14-square meters) across from the local newspaper office, where my father worked as a bookkeeper.[4]

There wasn't a school in the village so I had to go to school on a Sovkhoz seven kilometers away.[5] I stayed there in the school dormitory made up of two large rooms. At the beginning of the year both rooms were full, but after a month or so only several children remained. The boys played *ochko*, *bura*, and *kostyashki*, all for money, and I lost the 30 rubles my mother had given me to buy food in the cafeteria.[6] Once I learned how to play I was able to win back the 30 rubles, which I hid in order to have enough for food. This is how I lived that winter and spring.

During the holidays I worked in a silk winding factory, drying cocoons in a four-floor building. There were racks covered with tarps every meter-and-a-half. The racks were 50- to 60-meters long, and we moved across them by climbing on the racks. We turned the cocoons with both hands, then climbed to the next rack to do the same. We did this all day.

My father was transferred to the newspaper *Ferganskaya Pravda*, so he had to leave for Fergana. I went with him and attended the tenth grade in Fergana. We lived at the newspaper office and slept on the floor or in chairs. Not great conditions for studying, but I did okay.

I remember the first time I went to school in Fergana a girl invited me to sit at her table, where three other students were sitting. During a break one of the local boys grabbed me by the collar and wanted to hit me just because I was a Jew, though no one helped me. So I had to defend myself. Prior to this he'd beaten up another boy at my table who was also a Jew. Besides us, there were no other Jews in our class.

---

[4] 14-square meters is approximately 150-square feet.
[5] Sovkhoz was a state-owned farm in the Soviet Union.
[6] *Ochko* and *Bura* are card games; *kostyashki* is similar to pitching pennies.

I eventually became friends with the children and helped them study, and they defended me from anti-Semitism. At the end of the school year, as I was going down the stairs, that same boy came up behind me with a knife. But the military instructor grabbed him and twisted the knife away. I never saw the boy again.

The girl who sat beside me, Faya, could see that I was hungry and brought me lunch every day. She'd put it on the desk for me. Faya was doing better than us because her older sister had married a Red Army officer who supplied her family with food.

I went to Tashkent to enroll in the Voronezh Aviation Institute in 1943, but when I learned that the food ration card at Tashkent Railway Institute was better I went there. I tutored a student at the institute who helped me by giving me food. When I became sick from hunger, a doctor in Tashkent said that if I made it to spring I'd live. After three years in Tashkent I decided to return to Odessa in 1946. I enrolled at the Odessa Naval Institute to study ship mechanics.

I met my wife Luisa in Odessa in March 1951, and at the end of July I left for Baku, Azerbaijan, where I worked as a design engineer. Luisa and my mother came to Baku, where we registered our marriage. Four months later we celebrated our wedding when I went to Odessa for Luisa. I worked seven years in Baku, returning to Odessa with Luisa in 1957. Our daughter Galina was born in 1953, and nine years later our son Rudolf was born.

I worked at the Marine Sciences Engineering Institute as a designer and team lead for 35 years, and received 35 patents. Some of my designs were shown at the Exhibition of Achievements for National Economy, where I received five silver and four bronze medals over the years.

We immigrated to America soon after I retired in 1992. My daughter's family had immigrated in 1989. My two younger brothers immigrated to Israel, Ilya in 1977 and Israil in 1989.

Frida Chausovskaya

Ukraine

I was born in 1930 in Romny, Ukraine. Our city wasn't large, but it was very green with so many trees you couldn't tell the city from the woods. We lived just outside Romny in a small apartment over a bakery, so we were hot in the summer and warm in the winter. Our living conditions were poor and all of our amenities were outside, behind the barn. To bathe, we poured water from a spout can over each other.

We had just cleaned ourselves up before going for a walk on Sunday, June 22, 1941, when we heard a horrible noise. We didn't understand what was happening when the bombs exploded, but we soon heard the report over the radio that war had begun. German aircraft bombed our city several times a day, so we dug trenches and covered them with branches and other things to hide inside when the bombers came.

On September 10, 1941, after a typical bombing, a woman told us that a German tank division had entered the city. After dark, my mother, older sister and I crossed the bridge over the Sula River and hurried to a friend's house on the other side of the city to stay overnight.

My father hadn't returned from work, so our mother told us to hide in the woods while she went to search for him. They returned together and found me and my sister, who was crying hysterically. She was ten years older than me and emotionally unstable. Once they found us we all left for Sumy, walking three days and three nights. When we turned back to look, our city was in flames.

We decided to go to Voronezh on foot, about 400 kilometers away. We moved at night and hid during the day, staying with peasants along the way. The villagers thought of us in varying ways; in general, Ukrainians didn't like Jews, but there were some who invited us into their homes and fed us what they could. Along the way we ate carrots, beets, and potatoes from Kolkhoz fields that hadn't yet been harvested.[1] We asked the villagers to cook for us and shared the vegetables with them. All we had were the clothes on our backs, which we wore out on the way to Voronezh.

Trains with cattle cars were being readied to evacuate refugees from the Voronezh area, so we boarded one without knowing where it was going. We assumed it was headed for northern Kazakhstan. Our final stop was a village there, Ashkanat, where a woman let us live in one of her rooms. We worked on a Kolkhoz during the war, in poor conditions, and I also worked as a cleaning woman in the village.

Romny was liberated before the war ended, so my father said that we should return to our city. As our train arrived in Romny we were shocked to see the devastation. Our old neighbors told us my mother's brother and his wife were shot by the Germans on the eve of the war as they walked to a hospital. My uncle didn't even get to say goodbye to his son, who'd gone into the army as a tank driver. His training was cut short so the army could send him to the border before the war began. Two of my uncle's other sons were sent to the front as well. Our neighbors also told us what happened to the Jews who'd remained in the city. Many were shot or killed in other ways, and a group of young Jews was taken to Germany.

As I said, my sister Betya was not well. My mother took her out of school many times instead of finding treatment for her, and pleaded with teachers to advance her to the next grade. When they refused to advance Betya into the tenth grade, my mother decided to teach her a profession. She found someone to teach Betya accounting skills, and she could also type, so my sister was able to find work in a Zagotzerno laboratory before the war.[2]

There was someone living in our old home in Romny, but we were given a one-room apartment that had a kitchen and a toilet. Eventually my cousin, Sima, invited me to go to Rostov-on-Don, Russia, to live with her and her daughter and to attend the Railway Transportation Institute there. She told me the institute had dormitories for students and provided

---

[1] A Kolkhoz was a Collective Farm in the Soviet Union.
[2] A Zagotzerno was an organization devoted to grain procurement for bread.

scholarships, so I moved. Sima's husband, a Red Army colonel, had been killed in the war.

I moved to Rostov-on-Don and enrolled for my first year at the Railway Institute. The allotment of bread was 200 grams a day, but I also made some money as a porter at the train station.

I worked three years for the Perm Railroad in Russia's Ural region. Since I had free travel for vacations, I could visit my parents in Romny fairly often. During one visit I met Mikhail Rabinovich, a cadet at the Romny Military Automobile School. He later became my husband.

I couldn't find work in Romny, but my husband and I moved to Konotop, Ukraine, where he was stationed after he finished his schooling. We rented an apartment there and had our two sons, Aleksander and Pavel. Life wasn't easy in Konotop: I had to take Aleksander with me when I pumped water at five in the morning and when I chopped wood to heat our room. And still I worked, because my husband didn't make much and sent money to his family in Chernigov.

Aleksander completed the institute through correspondence courses and had to find work. He was told it was okay that he was Jewish but should change his name.[3] We decided to change our last name to Chausovsky.

In 1990 there were rumors of possible pogroms in Kiev, so my husband's boss put their unit at the highest readiness condition. We left for America in 1991 after Pavel and his family moved from New York to Tucson, Arizona. By the time we got here our grandson Valeriy was twelve years old. Natali, his little sister, was born in 1995. Life goes on, and you have to survive.[1]

---

[3] In the Soviet Union, Rabinovich (Ms. Chausovsky's son's last name) was used as a catchall name for Jews in anecdotes, jokes, and numerous other disparaging ways.

[1] Frida Chausovskaya passed away on January 19, 2014.

Erika Dattner

Hungary

I was born in Budapest, Hungary, on March 7, 1937, as Erika Berger.[1] My parents were Sophie (Zsofia in Hungarian) and Henrik Berger. My mother was a first-rate dressmaker, who learned her trade from her early teen years. She worked in an elegant salon in Budapest's elite shopping districts. My father was a tool and dye maker; he worked in the then well-known "Wertheimer" elevator factory. We were not rich but lived comfortably with two incomes.

My parents kept company for seven years before my father was allowed to marry, as his parents needed his income to support the family. Mother patiently waited (like Jacob for Rachel). Father had one brother and one sister. We had very little contact with this side of the family. Ultimately, I lost all contact with my father's family.

I came along four years after my parents were married. My paternal grandfather died three months before I was born. I was an only child.

My warmest and practically only recollection of my family was on my mother's side. My grandparents, Eduard-Elias and Anna Steiner, had seven offspring: three boys and four girls. Having lived in the Austro-Hungarian territory and given the difficult economic conditions of the time, my grandparents became "wandering Jews" throughout Germany and Austria, before they finally re-settled back in Hungary. Along the way, two children were born in Germany, one (my mother) in Vienna and the rest of the children in Hungary.

My grandparents were good, decent, hardworking people. Even though I barely remember my maternal grandmother, as she died when I was only three, I always think and reflect on her as a kind, loving person

---

[1] Reprinted with Ms. Dattner's permission from *120 HIAS Stories*, published in 2002.

like a mother hen . . . she came from a traditional Jewish background, whereas Grandpa was a totally secular person and a laborer. They barely spoke Hungarian; the language in their home was German, which all the children spoke fluently. One of the boys died as a young child and a sister as a young woman.

The years scattered the family: the two brothers left Hungary for France: one settled in Paris, the other in Algiers (then French territory) and moved to Nice in the '50s. One of the sisters moved to France before WWII, where she died. Out of the entire family only mother and one sister (Catherine) remained in Hungary with their parents. My aunt Catherine never married; she lived with her parents to the end and supported them. She became my closest – and almost only known – relative. She was intelligent and basically self-educated. She learned English before the war and I remember seeing *National Geographic* magazines in her home in the '30s. I recall, as a young child, enjoying the smell of the newsprint and looking at those wonderful pictures. She held an important position with a prominent firm; had a very nice, spacious apartment in the fashionable downtown part of the city, had a live-in maid/housekeeper to attend to her parents as well. She was a lady of society, frequented coffee houses, theatre, opera. She took me once to Lake Balaton, a famous resort area.

Life in pre-war Budapest flowed smoothly, in spite of some economic difficulties. Budapest was a cosmopolitan city, considered at the time to be the Paris of Eastern Europe. Most Jews in the city were assimilated and considered themselves as staunch Hungarians (just like the German Jews). Little by little, anti-Jewish laws were brought about. One of the laws called for Jewish men to enlist in order to serve in a Labor Battalion. These Labor Forces were annexed to the Hungarian army, to do their dirty work, like digging ditches and clearing minefields.

As the Hungarian army advanced toward Russia and the Eastern Front, with winter coming on, many of these men starved, froze, were abused or simply shot by their Hungarian superiors. My father, at age 37, was taken for forced labor and became one of these unfortunate victims . . . only because he was Jewish! My paternal grandmother received a notice, years later, from the Hungarian state department, claiming he "disappeared in Russian activity territory between 1941 and 1942 and was declared to have died a hero's death"! Hungary did not deserve him dying for her! We never heard from or about him again. I barely knew my father as I was only five when he was taken from us.

After father was taken away, mother had to take over being breadwinner and both mother and father. I was the only child in the small family, the apple of their eyes, but still very unspoiled. Children of my generation had to grow up fast, understand the conditions we were subjected to and mature faster than children in today's world. We were robbed of our childhood. We had no money to splurge on toys, dolls or frivolities. I remember asking my mother when I saw something I liked in a store window: "*Anyuka* (mommy) – will you buy it for me when you have money?" The answer, of course, was always "yes" . . . but it never came to pass.

Eventually, more anti-Jewish laws came about. One made all Jews wear the yellow star. Then, one that called for all Jews to be concentrated in one neighborhood, move into "Jewish Houses," or as they were called, "Star Houses." I was in first grade but I had to quit school; that was the total sum of my "education" in Hungary. We had to leave our home on a minute's notice, with only the small amount of personal belongings we could hand-carry. Luckily, we knew a family in that "Jewish district" who agreed to share their apartment with us; so mother, aunt, grandpa and I all moved in.

Conditions were getting harsher. Food shortages, curfews, bombings, fear, arrests. Every time we heard sirens, we had to rush down to the cellars. News started filtering in about the death camps. People were searching for ways to hide, if they were lucky. Mother and Catherine were among those lucky ones. They found false Christian ID papers and hid as housekeepers with Christian families. Grandpa was taken into the ghetto, where he survived the war. Mother found a place for me in a home for children whose fathers were taken to Forced Labor, organized by Protestant clergy. Here I was hidden throughout the war, under false names. I remember not having any fresh foods during this period, only dry staples like beans, peas, lentils, etc. As the Russians were advancing and the Germans retreating, Budapest got caught in the crossfires. Water lines were severed. During snowy days, we were taken outside and were able to eat the fresh snow, in lieu of fresh water. They also used it for cooking and sanitary uses. Speaking of sanitation: we had none. Many of us, including myself, developed skin sicknesses and lice.

During one of the bombing episodes our house was hit; debris, glass, beams, concrete all over us; we were all in panic and were rushed to the cellar; kids pushing each other. I slid on the stairs, head down, cut my head on glass, which left a scar where hair never grew again.

After liberation by the Russians, pedestrian, daytime movement was possible; however, evening curfews were still in effect. My mother was the first parent to show up to claim her child. She was taking me to her place of hiding, on foot. There was no motorized transportation; we had to walk. Darkness caught up with us; we needed to get indoors, but where?

After knocking on several doors and basement windows and not being accepted, although mother pleaded that she had a small child, we were luckily admitted to a small house where we spent the night: mother on a beach chair and I in a baby's crib. They also gave us a warm drink and a bite to eat. We were very grateful to be treated kindly and to be out of the dark and the cold street.

Eventually, people started coming out of hiding and the lucky ones who survived trickled back home, toward the city, searching for family members. Some of the bridges were destroyed between Buda and Pest. No transportation. People everywhere walking in hordes, carrying small satchels, bags, carts or bicycles. We managed to get to our old apartment only to discover that it was occupied by strangers; no one expected the Jews to survive and return to claim it and their possessions! We had nothing left but our lives and no place to live. We proceeded to my aunt's apartment. Luckily, we found her and grandpa alive. Their place was also settled by strangers but they were allowed to have one room.

Things were chaotic at this post-war city; buildings bombed out, food practically non-existent . . . we had nowhere to stay. Somehow, my mother found contact with a Zionist organization, where she was hired as a cook, in a home for teens. Conditions after liberation were so harsh that people turned into savages: dead horses left by the army were quickly cut up by the hungry hordes. Some food was left on farms outside the city (whatever was not taken by the Germans or the liberating Russian troops). People in the city, who had any valuables left or hidden, headed to the farms to exchange them for food. Trains were few and far between. The ones that did leave the city were jam-packed with people, baskets, suitcases heading to the farms. Those who could not get inside rode on top.

The organization mother joined also had a home for the younger children, where I was placed. We were told they would help us go to Palestine. Mother was fed up with Hungary after the way they treated us. We were given Hebrew names: She became Lea and I, Ora (light). We were smuggled out of Hungary in February, 1946, by train to Vienna. We had assumed identities (again!) and were taken to a transit station, which used to be a hospital; we were promptly fumigated with DDT (for lice, etc.) There were hundreds of refugees of various nationalities assembled there, speaking all languages of Babel! We were grouped with other Hungarians. After a few days, we were transferred to a DP camp in Germany, near the town of Ansbach, in Bavaria. This camp used to be a sanatorium named "Strüth." It had pleasant grounds, surrounded by shrubs and trees of all kinds. Children of similar ages were housed in barracks; couples were accommodated in rooms. The place, like many others all over Europe, were run and maintained by the American Joint Distribution Committee. Slowly, things got organized: school for children, sewing room, medical personnel, etc. Some of the original German maintenance personnel remained to tend the grounds. Meals were served in a communal dining room; we had occasional entertainment by our own talents.

All this while we were waiting for *aliyah* (immigration to Palestine). Mother got together here with a man who also had two teenage sons. We spent two long years in this camp. One day, mother and I visited some distant relatives in another city and upon our return discovered – to our astonishment – that the camp was empty! While we were gone, they made *aliyah*. After waiting all that time, we missed the boat!

Somehow, we were directed to another camp in the south of France, near Marseilles. From here we got a transport boat. It was a small fishing vessel; they built double bunks in its hull, where we were paired up for sleeping. It carried 200 people – we were packed like sardines, but we were on our way to Palestine! When we passed Cyprus, it flew the Turkish flag, so we managed to pass under the noses of the British unnoticed. It took us 12 long, arduous days from Marseilles to their shores of Palestine, which normally takes three. The Mediterranean in mid-November is no bowl of cherries, especially not in a tiny vessel. It was named quite appropriately: *Aliyah*. At last, at dawn on November 16, 1947, we arrived at the shores of Palestine; we anchored out at sea, near Nahariya (in the north) and were brought to shore with small rubber boats, in shifts. When mother stepped off the boat onto land, she knelt down and kissed the ground. We were welcomed by the *Haganah* (the Jewish underground personnel) and taken to several *kibbutzim*. By the time the British realized there was this illegal boat at the shore and seized it, all they caught was an empty ship.

After a few days in the *kibbutz*, we were sent to Rechovot, where we got an apartment. We had nothing but the clothes on our backs. Mother was able to get a job in an army camp as a cook. I was left with some new friends. I started school but my Hebrew knowledge was weak. Shortly thereafter, mother found the man she lived with in Germany. He wound up being on the ship *Exodus*, which was sent back to Germany, then ended up on Cyprus, and finally in a *kibbutz* in Israel. She bailed them out from the *kibbutz* after a quick marriage; exchanged our apartment in Rechovot for one in Haifa, where we got an old Arab apartment. The marriage lasted six years; it got rockier each year and ended in divorce. These were miserable years for me, living in a household with two older sons from another marriage. I was treated like Cinderella.

In 1948, the state was formed and became Israel. Again, tough times, rationing of basic staples, primitive conditions (like cooking on petroleum lamps, leaking iceboxes). People thrown together from many countries, speaking many languages with varied cultures. None of the conveniences we take for granted today. Israel was a poor, up and coming country, fighting for its existence. It was very hard to make a living.

Around this time, my aunt Catherine immigrated to the U.S., after grandpa passed away. Mother applied for a visa too, which was a lengthy procedure. Because of the family problems, she sent me (at age 17) to my uncle in Paris, hoping I could get to America from there, when she got her visa, thereby avoiding the army service in Israel. Well, things turned out differently. The French would not extend my visitor's visa and Israel demanded my return to serve in the army. So, I became a soldier at 18. During this time, mother's visa came through, which would have expired if not acted upon. She had to leave me and sail to America to join her sister. She had a tough time making ends meet, and I was left alone in Israel. During this time I met someone, Tibor-Zeev Goldstein, who later became my husband and father of our two daughters, Sara and Michelle.

Sometime after being released from my two-year army service (which I ended as sergeant), I followed mother to the U.S. I arrived in 1957 on the *S.S. United States*, which was the fastest ship in the world. It was an awesome feeling seeing the Statue of Liberty in person! I couldn't believe I was actually in New York. HIAS was very helpful at this critical time for me; a representative met me on board, whizzed me through the maze of red-tape of immigration, customs and the general confusion of it all. She accompanied me off the ship to the happy arms of my mother and aunt.

It was not easy adjusting to the new homeland: economically, socially, etc. I felt quite lonely and lost. I "imported" my husband-to-be, after marrying him in Israel. The marriage lasted 22 years and ended in divorce. I am now remarried to Kurt Dattner, who is a survivor as well as a hidden child himself.[2] After 42 years in New York, I moved with him to Tucson, where the sun always shines. We have seven grandchildren between us, unfortunately much too far away. Reflecting on my life, I know I was handed the short end of the "stick" and I only hope for the leftover years in good health, and hopefully peace!

---

[2] Kurt Dattner was born in Germany and escaped to Belgium, where he was hidden in a Catholic orphanage and a Protestant school. Kurt passed away on July 20, 2012.

Theresa Dulgov

Hungary

I was born in Hungary in June 1944, the month after the Germans entered the country to deport the Jews.[1] They'd already taken certain people to work for them – like my father – to use as human shields and slave labor. When the Germans attacked the Soviet Union, the Hungarians went in first and the Germans followed after. Hungarian Jews were the first to be killed when there were skirmishes.

Jews were also used as forced labor by the Germans. They would be taken away for months, return for a few months, then be sent away again. My father was used in this way, along with many other Jews. But the actual camp deportations didn't begin until sometime around April or May 1944, when the Germans began picking up Jews and taking them away on trains.

My father was a farmer and had quite a bit of land. The Germans would arrive at the farm when he wasn't at home and destroy various things in the house. Whatever couldn't be taken was destroyed. They even urinated in my mother's piano.

My father's prized possessions were the beautiful white show horses he trained, but when the Germans came they overworked the horses. They would hitch them to carts and ride them hard, which killed the horses. They weren't bred to do these things.

My mother was very pregnant and decided to go to Budapest, where her mother was. The Germans knew people were moving around and watched the stations carefully. You couldn't travel by train without someone checking your papers to see if you were Jewish. But as Hungarian guards approached to check her out, my mother pretended to

---

[1] Ms. Dulgov is the daughter of Eva Siebert, whose story is also featured in this collection.

be in labor. German SS officers on the train took care of her, so the Hungarians couldn't do anything. When the train reached Budapest, the SS officers helped her off and flagged down a taxi for her so she could get to a hospital. As soon as the station was out of sight, my mother went to her sister's house instead, where my grandmother was. My mother was lucky that day: she boarded a train with sympathetic Germans onboard.

She went into labor and went to a hospital where a friend of hers worked. There was an air raid in the middle of her labor, so they held her back from having me and took her to the hospital's shelter. She couldn't continue with the labor, so they performed a C-Section to save me.

My mother's father was a lawyer who'd apparently done a special thing during World War I that allowed him certain privileges. He didn't have to wear the yellow star, while my mother did. This was a very rare thing, and the hopes were that these privileges extended to my mother as well. She soon found that they did not; the Germans came after her.

They took my grandmother away a few weeks after I was born. Budapest wasn't a safe place to be because the Jews had to live in certain areas, in ghettos. My paternal grandmother lived in a ghetto, as did my father's sister.

My maternal grandmother lived in another ghetto, and my mother begged her one day not to return there. My mother was just twenty-six years old and had a new baby, her first child. But my grandmother said she had to care for her own sister, who was blind. That same night the Germans took her from the ghetto. My mother always had this terrible feeling she didn't do everything she could for her mother.

After that, my mother had nowhere to go. She couldn't stay with her parents, and although she knew my father's parents were in the ghetto, she wasn't sure where. So she went into hiding.

At one point the Germans actually picked my mother up, but she was able to escape. She and I had been put with a group of Jews and were on our way to a train station when a ruckus of some sort occurred. My mother slipped out of the group with me in her arms and hid beneath a bridge. She stood knee-high in water until they'd taken everyone else away. Again she was so lucky; no one in line said anything, and my mother was able to keep her baby (me) quiet as she hid.

Hours later, very late at night, she came out from under the bridge. It was sometime in September, and she was soaking wet. She went to a place that we'd now call a safe house, where she met with Rauol Wallenberg.[2] He was going to get her papers to keep her safe, though that would take some time to do. In the meantime, she had to find food for her and her baby.

Eventually, she couldn't return to the safe house any longer, but she knew there was a Catholic convent nearby and went there to ask the nuns for help. They told her that if she promised to have her child baptized and raised as a Catholic, they would let her stay there. My mother agreed. I was baptized, and the nuns allowed us to stay in the convent's attic, which had a large window. At first this worked out, but in the winter it became a big problem. There was no heat in the attic, and the window was open with snow and the wind coming in.

The nuns were hiding another Jewish woman with two children up there as well. My mother and the woman would walk to the Danube river each day to fetch water for us. One would scoop up the water and hand it up the bank to the other. While they were at the river one day, a soldier shot and killed the other woman while she scooped water. My mother ran back to the convent, where the children were. After that she didn't like leaving me at the convent when she went for water. She said that if she died, so would I. From then on, when she went for water, she wrapped me in a sheet and hung the sheet around her neck. She never left me alone after that incident.

She soaked beans in water to eat, cooked them, then put the beans in a cloth diaper for me to suck on. She cooked potato peels and put them in the diaper as well. By the time the war was over I'd lost weight and had a huge belly. I was constantly hungry. I have bone issues because of malnutrition and no milk. After the war, my mother would take me from the convent to a nearby Russian camp, where one of the soldiers loved to see me. He would save his lunch for my mother, and told her he'd always have a slice of bread and some soup for the baby. My mother returned to

---

[2] Raoul Wallenberg was a Swedish diplomat who saved tens of thousands of Jews in Nazi-occupied Hungary during World War II. He was detained by the Soviets after the war and is reported to have died in the Lyubyanka prison in Moscow.

the Russian camp each day. It saved my life.

My father returned from the front after Hungary was under the control of the Russians. They considered my parents to be *kulaks*, because they still owned half of their land.[3] When my father returned, he tried to get the farm back but was unsuccessful. We lived in town for a short time, then went to stay at my father's vineyard until it was taken away. My father was taken to jail in 1950 for being a so-called *kulak*, so my mother decided to go to Budapest, where my paternal grandmother lived, to see if she could make a better life there. It was also closer to the prison where my father was being held. My sister was born in 1946, so my mother had two daughters with her, six and four years old. My father got out of jail at some point that year.

When the Hungarian Revolution took place in 1956, my father was in the hospital with a skin disease. He entered the hospital in February, and died in November that year. I always say is was the Hungarian uprising that killed him.

My mother realized there was nothing left for us in Hungary and decide that we should go to America. We told people we were going to visit the farm, then caught a train going elsewhere after saying goodbye to my grandmother.

The Russians stopped all trains to check papers and to ask people where they were going. We had nothing to show them, so we got off the train at a village and stayed there overnight. The villagers told us what direction to take to the border, and after a few days walking we made it to a farmhouse we'd been told about.

There were a lot of people gathered at the farm, all headed for the border. They split us in two groups, ours with 16 and the other with 15 people. I had an old watch, and my sister carried a bottle of vodka in her bag. Our mother told her that if we were caught to give the vodka to the Russian soldiers. We had to pay a lot of money to get across the border, but my mother had sold our apartment – and everything we had – to ensure we had enough.

We left at night, walking from one haystack to another, until someone

---

[3] *Kulak* is a Tsarist Russian term for affluent farmers, expanded during Soviet rule to include nearly any peasant landowner. The Soviet government approved the extermination of *Kulaks* as a class in early 1930.

pointed at a small light in the distance. They said that was the other side of the border. The long walk was very difficult for my mother and me. Someone had gone ahead of us and given the Russians alcohol, and by the time we got there they were very happy. They even told their barking dogs to be quiet because they didn't see anything.

Austrians picked us up at about four in the morning. We found out from them that we'd traveled the longest possible way to get there, and that a crying baby in the other group had alerted the Russians to them. They were all caught. The Austrians took us to a small town, and each night after, we moved closer and closer to Vienna. Other people were arriving every night. By the time we got to Austria, my feet were so swelled up that I couldn't remove my shoes. I still have the one bag I carried on my back into Austria.

We left Hungary on December 6, 1956, and didn't arrive in America until December 16, 1958, due to all the refugees trying to do the same thing. We tried going to Portugal to get out, but we didn't realize there was a quota system for visas and couldn't leave from there either.

In Austria, I was at an age when I should have been in the eighth grade, so I had to catch up. By the time we arrived in America, I'd missed so much school that I had to return to the eighth grade. I didn't speak English yet, so I was always a year behind.

Annique Dveirin

Poland

My name is Annique Dveirin, although legally it's Ann because I became a citizen with that name. I was born Hania Beer, in Brzuchowice, Poland. We were part of Poland, but in an area where everyone spoke Ukrainian. Eventually that area became part of Ukraine. As I understand it, once the area became independent Ukraine, or during the Russian occupation, they changed the name to Boykovitso. My parents were Abram and Ruzia Beer.

We were six people living together in a three-room house: my parents, my father's brother and sister, my little sister, and me. I slept in a cradle, my aunt slept next to her sewing machine in a daybed, my parents had the big bed, my uncle had the other room, and there was a kitchen. In the winter they often cooked in the corner of the big room, which created enough heat that it was sort of central heating for the house. There was a big baking oven in the kitchen that had a place on top, and I remember sitting up there watching my mother and aunt bake.

My earliest experience with the Holocaust was shortly before the Germans occupied Poland. The locals knew the Germans were coming, and they began attacking us. I was three years old, and one night I woke in the middle of the night to people pounding at our door yelling, "Jews! Open up!" I overheard my parents saying to put the two-month-old baby to the breast so she wouldn't make noises while my aunt wrapped me in her shawl so the two of us could escape out the back window.

There was a river that ran through the village, and my aunt crossed the bridge with me. We went to a local Russian orthodox minister's house. In that region there was either Catholic or Russian orthodox, and since he was married he must have been orthodox. My aunt took me to a back bedroom to let me sleep, but suddenly someone knocked. They must have seen us coming. My aunt put me on her back again and we went out the back window. A young man was milling about near the bridge, so we swam the river. On the other side, I could see our house in the distance with a big bonfire burning out front. Peoples' shadows passed the bonfire, and they were throwing items into it. Then I went to sleep.

My aunt became startled, which woke me up. There was a big well in the village square for those who didn't have wells on their property, and there was a very tall man standing at the well in the night, which turned out to be my uncle. I don't remember when we returned to the house, but I remember that it was very empty. My parents' bed was stripped, and for the next few weeks my mother was busy plucking feathers for feather beds.

The friends I used to play with suddenly started calling me a dirty Jew, or a stinking Jew. Some threw rocks, and my father would chase them off. The police came for my father once, and the next day, when he came home, he was swollen from being beaten. And then the Germans came.

I had a dog named Totus that looked like a cocker spaniel. He always slept under my crib, and when the Germans came they shot my dog when he barked. They sent my uncle to get the cattle from the pasture, and his dog followed him, a Siberian Husky looking dog. At some point, the Germans shot at my uncle, but the dog jumped and was hit by the bullet. This was my first acquaintance with the Germans.

Our family changed during this time, everyone was very tense. There was a lot of whispering. I think they were trying to figure out if we would survive, because shortly after that, in the middle of the night, there was knocking at the door. It was Nikolai Kuzhmakh, who my parents said had once babysat me. My parents wrapped me up and handed me to Nikolai. We drove through the woods at night, to Nikolai's mother's house in the smaller village of Plytenice, which a man from the United States Holocaust Museum told me is now called Plotonitsa. It's no longer a part of Poland.

Mariya, Nikolai's mother, and his two younger brothers Vasiliy and Fedko were waiting up for us. The brothers were ten and twelve years old. Mariya had a daughter, Hanka, a husband, and a son named

Mechanko, who was over twenty years old. The husband and Mechanko worked for the Germans, but because I was a blue-eyed blond child I was passed off as being Hanka's illegitimate child of a German soldier. She quietly took me to church, and I was baptized by a priest. So I became Hanka Kuzhmakh.

Most of the time I stayed inside the house. I had to learn new prayers and a new identity. I was confused, but after a bit I answered to Hanka. At first people smiled, and nobody was too tense. But no one had said I'd never see my home again, for the rest of my life, or my family as I knew it. I cried many days once I realized I wasn't going back.

The house was one room, with a dirt floor and a cobbler's bench under the window. I slept on top of the baking oven, Russian style, which forced Vasiliy to the family bed, and when I cried Fedko would say, "Give her back, she doesn't want to be here!" I remember that their mother, Mariya, said I had a right to cry, that I'd lost everything.

I lived with them four years, and never went to school. I had chores to do, such as following after Mariya when she was hired out to cut wheat with a scythe. I would pick up any stalks that fell, and give them to her before she tied the sheath to put on a horse-drawn cart or a truck, depending on whose field it was. There was a well in the yard and fields that the boys ploughed in the summer. Mariya would poke at the ground with a big pole, and I'd put beans in the holes and cover them, or half a potato with the root down. As I got a little bigger I'd take the cattle to pasture: two cows, two horses, some sheep and goats.

Washing the boys shirts at the river one day, I watched as an airplane flew overhead. It was very low, and I could see a man who was pointing what looked like a rifle at me. The boys had taught me to swim, and when I saw that gun I jumped in the river and swam across. The funny thing is that I didn't wonder why that man was wasting bullets on a child washing clothes on a rock; I wondered how it was he could tell I was born Jewish. These things become a part of you.

Fedko would often beat me, so the only way to survive was to stay close to his mother. I remember when I left home that my mother had told me to be a good girl, so I always tried to do that. One day Fedko said he was going to tell the Germans I was Jewish. His mother came out of the kitchen and told him they'd take all of us, because they'd taken me in.

This was the beginning of my realization that I had some balance, that I had a way to defend myself. When Fedko hit me hard, I took a broomstick to him. I got a couple of knocks in. And this was my life there.

One day I noticed that the family was doing something in the barn, digging a hole. I soon realized that my aunt was living there as well, the same aunt that I'd lived with at home.

Mechanko and Mariya's husband came home from working with the Germans, and I think they worked in a concentration camp. Though I'd learned my prayers and all the things to do for church, there came a time when Mariya and I kneeled down to pray for the souls of her husband and Mechanko. I asked if they knew their prayers, and she said they did, but that we'd pray for their souls anyways. I didn't know about the camps, but I knew there were some sorts of prisons. And then Mechanko came home.

Mechanko was a cobbler. He worked at home and would go out drinking with his friends at night. Some of them showed up one night and hauled my aunt out of her hiding spot. I was huddling on top of the oven. The sounds of that night stayed with me forever; I knew the exact moment they murdered her.

Mariya sent the boys to dispose of the body, and after that I constantly looked for signs of fresh digging. Mechanko left with those men two days later. They were presented as partisans who supposedly fought the Germans, but all they did was hunt Jews. Whenever he'd come home to visit, Mechanko would fire his gun twice at the river, and Mariya would push me out of the house and tell me to stay out. I stayed in the cornfield, and slept there as well.

Another day, I went with Mariya to the post office in the village to see if her husband sent her money. On the way back, a skinny man and a short man asked Mariya if her son Nikolai was friends with Beerko in Brzuchowice.[1] When she said yes, the men scoffed and said that the whole family was gone. I wondered what would happen to me, but I wasn't allowed to cry when they bragged about killing Jews.

All sorts of scary things would happen. Once a German said I had Jewish eyes, and I skipped away until I was out of sight and then ran

---

[1] "Beerko" is a diminutive for of Ms. Dveirin's family name, Beer.

home. I also heard Germans talking about peasants hiding cattle and pigs, and that the Army needed food, so I told Mariya this. I remember that one morning I didn't hear a thing, no people or even cows mooing. The world was too quiet, something wasn't right. I didn't want to take the cattle to the pasture, so Mariya made Fedko take them. Two hours later, there were bullets everywhere, big cannons on the main dirt road, Russian *Katyushas* spitting huge shells.[2] The Germans were retreating and the Russians were coming.

Mariya took Vasiliy and me to a house with a basement, and a few hours later the people there were hungry, so Mariya sent me home for cheese and bread. I was walking between trucks and soldiers, and bullets, but when I tried to cross the road to her house something hit me in the hand and I bled and bled. I have a scar where it entered and exited. A Russian soldier came and looked at my hand, picked me up, and said that I looked like his daughter and that he'd take care of the bleeding. They cleaned me up at a medical truck, and the man gave me a nickname: *kurnosaya*, which means "short nose."

The man told me to stay at the truck, and that he'd come back for me after the fighting. So I did. He left soup for me in the tin can attached to his belt. He asked me to show him where I lived, and I took him. There were two or three women there who looked upset, so he went in. When he came out, he told me that when Fedko was out in the field with the cattle they'd run into the woods because of the bullets. Fedko was hit in the stomach, and was going to die. Mariya asked me to come in and pray for Fedko, and gave me my rosary. I said whatever prayers I knew, though I had no idea what forgiveness meant. Fedko died that night and was buried next to the village church. And we were liberated.

The next day, when I went for water at the well, I tripped over a young German man in the grass who kept asking for water. So I unhooked the ladle from the well and tried to put water in his mouth. He said, "mutti," which is mommy in German, then his head fell back and he died. I told Mariya that there was a dead German at the well, and she sent Vasiliy to tell the Russians. The Russians were not long on patience and she didn't want them to think we had hidden a German soldier.

---

[2] *Katyusha* was the name of a Soviet rocket launcher system used in World War II.

Several months later I found out that my father had survived. I found this out from a book that I read. They'd built a sort of underground bunker in the woods and stocked it, thinking the war would be over in two years. It took four. Of course, people get sick in winter, and they coughed enough that they thought the villagers may have heard them. My father and two first cousins, who later immigrated to Israel, went to look for a new hiding place. When they returned, all the others had been stripped naked and were murdered with axes and knives. My father and his cousins found over 60 bodies there. My mother was one of them. I don't think my father ever recovered from that. He and the two others joined another bunker of Jews in hiding. I met a woman in Israel who'd been in that group. She told me they had very little food, but they took my father and the two others in. She married one of the cousins after the war.

Once we joined with our father, we moved more towards the center of Poland, away from that section of Ukraine that we were in. In Bielsko-Biala he put us in an orphanage. My sister had something on her lungs, so she was taken somewhere, but came back cured.

My sister had been given to a woman they would hire to help with laundry when my mother was pregnant. The woman was Polish, not Ukrainian, and she had three children plus my sister. But the Ukrainians attacked the woman's home, and she ran off with her children, leaving my sister behind. A beggar took my sister in to get better alms, and the nuns recognized that the child wasn't his. She was baptized Zosia Przebylska, and my father tracked her down. The nuns denied having anyone that young, but afterward he went back and found my sister. He put her in his backpack, and even though the police shot at him he made it out.

Most of the children in the Bielsko-Biala orphanage were from Auschwitz. From there, our father told me to bring my sister, and to bring all our warm clothes to meet him at the train station. He was arrested just as we were boarding, as the police were looking for hidden money. Once my father caught up with us, we could see that the hems of his clothing were torn from the police search. I made it on the train, and when they asked for papers on the Czechoslovakian border I told them my mother had them and had gone to the toilet. In Prague they arrested a whole bunch of people and put them on trucks. They tried to arrest me, but I said I was waiting for my mother long enough for the truck to leave. I asked at the station which train was going west, and we got on it.

They caught up with us just before we made it to the French border, but I can't remember how we got through that. We wound up as refugees in Paris, and my sister and I went to an orphanage where all the schooling was done in Hebrew. My father wanted us to go to America, and in the meantime we lived in Fublaines, Verneuil, and Pontault-Combault.

Finally, our visas came through. I was fourteen years old when we arrived in Denver, Colorado. By then, my father was wiped out. I knew in America I needed an education, and worked very hard to get one, which is why I like to wear my Phi Beta Kappa Society pin.

Walter Feiger

Poland

I was born in Krakow, Poland, into a privileged family from the upper middle class. My father had a degree in chemistry from the University of Vienna, and my family owned a small factory that produced household products. In my early years I actually had two mothers: my maternal mother and our housekeeper, Marta, who was my governess. My mother was a socialite, so wherever Marta went I went with her. Marta was a devout Catholic, so on Sundays she took me with her to church. The Priest knew me by my first name, and every time I was there he put holy water on my head. Maybe that helped me to survive, because it's good to have two angels with you when you're in the death camps.

My early recollection is that the war between Poland and Germany officially began on September 1, 1939. I turned twelve on September 8, and my father had promised he'd be there for my birthday. He called to say he could not be there because he'd been called up into the army and had to report immediately. He served as an officer in the Austrian Army during World War I. That was the last time I had the opportunity to talk with my father, a few days before my twelfth birthday. Soon enough, the German Army entered the area we lived in.

We had moved out of Krakow, where I was born, and were living closer to the German border in a town called Katowice, Kattowitz in German. We lived in a nice apartment, and when German officers visited our place they decided they wanted to make their headquarters there. We were required to leave. All we could take was one suitcase apiece, with personal belongings, when we moved into a ghetto in a smaller town.

Katowice belonged to Germany before World War I, and when the

German occupation started they said they were reunifying greater Germany. Jews were no longer allowed to live in that area. We went to live with relatives in Chrzanow, located between Katowice and Krakow, just 18 kilometers from Auschwitz. You could see the chimneys working hard later on, when the weather permitted.

Every male over the age of twelve had to work for the Germans in some capacity. In my family, that meant my father and brother had work. My brother was three years older than me. At the age of seventeen, the Germans sent him to a Forced Labor Camp. My mother, fearing that I might have to go next, took me to a work command that repaired highways and canals. She thought that if I worked there they might not send me to Germany. One day, as we returned from work, we were ordered to go to a local gymnasium. We had to undress there and stand in front of German officials and doctors. In the meantime, SS Storm Troopers circled the building.

Officially, you had to be seventeen years old to be sent to Germany, and I wasn't quite fifteen. But the doctor said I was strong enough and should be sent to a camp. We were marched to the railroad station, where my mother was able to give me a small suitcase with personal belongings and some German marks. She was originally born and raised in Cologne, Germany, and had some connections with the local German police department.

Eight months after I was sent to the camp, the town we lived in was liquidated. All the Jews in the ghetto there were required to gather at the marketplace, where a commission of German officers and doctors ordered them to undress. The women, children and senior citizens were automatically sent to Auschwitz and gassed. Younger, physically fit people were sent to labor camps. My mother was just thirty-eight years old and spoke perfect German, but she was sent to Auschwitz. Since I was just fifteen years old, my destiny would have likely been the same as my mother's. Once you got to Auschwitz, you didn't last very long.

At first, we were sent to a transitional camp in Poland. There, I went to see an official, a *Kapo*, to ask if I could be sent to the same camp in Germany where my brother was.[1] I told him that if he could send me

---

[1] A *Kapo* was a prisoner assigned by the SS in Nazi prison camps to supervise forced labor or carry out administrative tasks.

there I would give him all the German money I had. I got lucky: he was able to send me to Sakrau, which was in Kreis Oppeln, Germany. I can still see the expression on my brother's face when he saw me coming in. He would have never dreamed in his wildest imagination that his fifteen-year-old brother would show up at that camp.

The first thing we had to do in the camp was undress. The Germans checked our clothing and confiscated our money and jewelry. We had to wear a yellow star indicating we were Jews. Normally, in the ghetto, you just sewed it on your shirt. But in the camp we had to cut the shirt and sew the star on top to keep you from escaping. We then had to go to what they called *entlausung*.[2] They apparently thought we all had parasites and lice, so we had to get rid of them. They sprayed us with chemicals.

They shaved our heads, very close to a crew cut, and we had to get up early in the morning to assemble in front of the barracks for a headcount. If everyone was present, we were dismissed. Back in the barracks, we would wash up and get our bread rations. We received a half pound of bread a day and an imitation cup of coffee, called ersatz café, mostly chicory with no real coffee in it. That was supposed to last us until we returned to the camp.

We mostly performed highway work at that camp. The Germans needed good highways to efficiently move their military equipment and units. The work was very hard, but I was lucky that I'd learned how to use a shovel when I lived at home. I also spoke perfect German because that was my first language. My mother spoke to us in German. People with no experience like that soon became a joke to the Germans, and were beaten and insulted. Those people deteriorated much faster than the rest.

In the first labor camps there were no other nationalities or religions besides Jews. At the very beginning there were even a few females that would work in the kitchen. When we returned from work late in the evening, we would get a bowl of soup. That was our entire nourishment for the day. Most of the time the soup had cabbage in it, or potato peels. There was never any meat in it, except on Hitler's birthday, when they gave us chowder. That was the only time we had something different.

---

[2] Delousing.

Obviously, we deteriorated physically due to malnutrition. Every once in a while someone would just give up because he couldn't handle it. One of the worst possible punishments is starvation. If you have experienced starvation – I don't mean being hungry from one day to another, but real starvation – you know it's something that doesn't happen immediately. Your body deteriorates, and your mind preoccupies itself with one thing: food. You come to a point where you're demoralized, nothing really matters. Your only thought is: "how can I get some food?" Believe me, this is one of the worst feelings that you can have. Anything that moved would be eaten. You couldn't find any cockroaches because that was food.

We had a nine o'clock curfew, and after that we weren't allowed out of the barracks. There was a large pot to use for going to the bathroom. We slept on bunk beds without mattresses, just straw. We were punished for everything: wet spots near the bathroom pot and loose straw under our beds led to severe beatings. Life wasn't easy in a labor camp; the worst was still to come once the labor camps were liquidated in 1943.

Coming back from work one day we were told that we were going to be moved to concentration camps. I remember at one place I would occasionally see a truckload of men in stripes, and I knew they were from the concentration camps. We had to undress and stand in front of the commission again. Those who were weak were sent to the left, and those the Germans felt were still able to work were sent to the right.

You never wanted to end up in the infirmary. If you did, you could last a day or two, but the SS would conduct inspections in the infirmary and send everyone there to Auschwitz, or to some other neighboring camp that had ovens. I had an infection on the bottom of my foot once that I cut out with a piece of glass. I never wanted to go to the infirmary; I knew I'd never come out if I did.

On the night the labor camp was liquidated, we marched about eight kilometers in columns of 50 to Gross-Rosen concentration camp. There was one SS officer in front of us and one in back, both with rifles loaded. It was wintertime, and it was snowing. I became panicked and had severe pains in my stomach just looking at the camp. Gross-Rosen had double-barbed wire in three lines: one in front, one in between, and one about 30 feet farther out. The inside line of barbed wire was electric, so if you approached it you got electrocuted. There were towers with machine gun mounts every few hundred yards, and SS officers walking around with dogs that were ready to rip you apart.

In the concentration camp there were people of all nationalities: Poles, Russians, Frenchmen, Italians, Greeks, Gypsies, Jehovah's Witnesses, and even Germans. The conditions were very difficult. Every barracks had 600 members with a *Kapo* in charge of it and his assistant. Inspections were conducted day and night. I hid a piece of glass so I could shave whenever I could, because when they had inspections and they found unshaved areas you would get 50 lashes. Very few people survived the lashes, because they were done with iron covered in leather. The *Kapos* administered the punishment with all their force. I was lashed once and couldn't sit for a long time. It penetrated your skin.

Sunday was our day off, but they would make us carry piles of debris from one place to another, then clean the old area up. When you were finished, they made you take the pile to its original location. They were trying to demoralize us. They made us wear striped uniforms that looked like pajamas but were harsh on the skin. We didn't have underwear, so in the winter we froze. There were fires, but only for the Germans.

In the morning assembly, the people that had died during the night were piled on top of each other. I remember two Russian prisoners arguing over a piece of soap until a *Kapo* hit them and they fell on the floor. He pressed his boots on each of their throats until they died. This became routine. We became so accustomed to death and dying that it stopped meaning anything. The survival ratio was very small. My brother and I hung on and helped each other; we did what we could.

Then things got worse. The Russians were getting closer to Bavaria and the Germans feared being captured by them. We had to evacuate, which became the so-called "death march." Those who couldn't keep up were shot. Most of the SS soldiers in the camp were Ukrainian; they couldn't speak German, but they hated Jews with a passion.

We walked and walked, and people were shot. When someone fell down and couldn't get back up he was shot. We spent our nights in horse stalls full of infection and horse lice that caused typhus. My brother was one of the unfortunates; he wound up with typhus and died in my arms, six weeks before the liberation. This was the worst for me. My brother and I had managed to be together for over three years, and now I no longer had the desire to live. There was no reason for me to survive.

But somehow I did. One day I went down to the barracks and the guards were gone. Before we knew it, a battalion of Polish soldiers entered the camp and told us we were free. They interviewed us and set us free. That was easier said than done, because most of us, like me, were just skin and bones. I was in no condition to go anywhere.

If I had been liberated by the allies, I would have been sent to a Displaced Persons camp and received clothing, medical care, and food. Since I was on the Russian side, I had to care for myself.

Going back to Poland wasn't easy, because there little transportation to be had. Trains at the time could travel about 50 kilometers, but then you'd have to find another one. I had a suitcase full of things I'd acquired, but every time we stopped Russians soldiers would inspect us. By the time I got to Poland, my suitcase was empty.

When I arrived in Poland I was arrested for wearing German clothes, and they thought maybe I was part of the *Hitlerjugen*.[3] They checked my documents and released me.

Nobody else came home, and there was nobody there. I found out where my old governess lived; she'd gotten married since I left. I visited with her and we cried together. Then I found out Poles in a neighboring town had killed a dozen Jews. I couldn't understand that; my father was an officer in the Polish Army, and I was born in Poland. I considered myself Polish. It turned out that the Poles who killed those Jews now owned the Jews' old homes and stores, and weren't willing to give them up. I really didn't feel safe there anymore; it seemed safer to return to Germany. So I went back to Germany.

In Germany, I joined the Palestinian Jewish Legion, a Zionist organization. I was smuggled to the American side in Europe and eventually went to Marseilles, France, to wait transportation to Palestine. There were 600 of us on a boat made for 50, and when we arrived at Haifa, Palestine, the English turned us away because the camps were over capacity there. We went to Cyprus, and I joined the Israeli underground. I was finally released to go to Palestine, where I worked for

---

[3] The Hitler Youth was a paramilitary organization of the Nazis made up of German males aged 14-18.

awhile in construction then went into the Israeli Army as a Lieutenant.

Not long after that, I decided to move back to France, where I met and married my first wife. When President Eisenhower created a special "political refugee" category for Holocaust Survivors, my wife and I moved to America. I say: G-d Bless America.

Yulia Genina

Ukraine

My twin sister and I were born in Kharkov, Ukraine, on September 28, 1930. She lives in Cleveland, Ohio. In the 1930s our family was very poor, but after my parents received their own apartment we lived comparatively well. My father bought a piano, and I studied music from the age of six. I was a good student, and received good grades. Everything was going well until the war suddenly began.

Because Kharkov was such an industrialized city there were many major factories there, such as the tractor factory which also made tanks and other military equipment. The Germans bombed Kharkov quite soon after the war began, although the Germans were still fairly far away. Our father kept us calm as a panic broke out in the city. He was born in 1891, and his village had been occupied by the Germans during World War I. He said that the Germans were intelligent and cultured, and that they wouldn't treat people poorly or kill the Jewish people. He said they didn't do this in World War I and they wouldn't now. This calmed our family quite a bit.

My sister and I were ten years old and our father was fifty, so he wasn't sent to the front. He was called up instead into the civil defense army that dug trenches and other things to slow the enemy down. The civil defense army sent him somewhere, though we weren't sure where he was.

The Germans started bombing Kharkov right away. All across the city, homes were either completely destroyed or on fire. It was simply horrible. In just over three months the Germans occupied Kharkov, in October 1941.

Prior to that the trains continued to move. Kharkov was an industrial center and the government had to evacuate factory equipment to safer locations to continue making weapons.

Soon after the Germans entered Kharkov, my mother went to get groceries and saw an announcement that the Jews, to include the children, had to gather quite far from the city at the tractor factory with their money, gold and other valuables. That's when my mother began to panic. She sewed small pouches from fabric to use as backpacks so we could take a few small things, and we left Kharkov.

We headed east, moving for quite some time from village to village. At first people helped us, but then it became very dangerous for them to do so. Nazi soldiers were going door to door searching. We always heard their dogs barking, so we were alerted. We would stay in cellars when people let us; everyone was in fear for their lives and some were afraid to let us stay. We were fearful as well.

We decided to cross the front, though I don't recall very much of that. I remember that we went through the woods at night to get to the Soviet side. This was extremely dangerous to do because the front wasn't a straight line and was always changing. But we made it.

Someone told my mother a train with factory equipment was heading east. We made it to that particular station, but the train had machinery on flat cars and several boxcars, but no wagons for people to sit in. The boxcar doors were closed, so we sat down on the station platform. It was October, so it was cold. Someone saw us and opened a boxcar door, then helped us in. There were already people inside the boxcar.

The train moved very slowly. Near Belgorod (less than 200 kilometers from Kharkov), we heard the distended noise of a German Messerschmitt, which everyone recognized, and the earth all around us began to explode. People in the boxcar yelled that we should jump out and scatter, that if a bomb hit the boxcar everyone would be killed.

Through cracks in the boxcar we could see two small children crying and running around a woman whose body was lifeless on the ground. Our mother put us on her lap and hugged us, saying, "if our fate is to survive we survive together. I don't want to live without you, and I don't want you to be left without me." The sound of that Messerschmitt has been in my mind since that day. I will never forget seeing the pilot in his cockpit, which was open, flying low and spraying those who had jumped from the boxcar with his machine guns. Afterwards, our train continued on, though slowly.

The second time we were bombed was after we passed Kursk. The rail route was one that existed long ago and went to Crimea, Kharkov, Moscow via Belgorod, Kursk, Tula, and Moscow. As we passed Kursk the Germans attacked the train, but the train was moving very fast and there were no casualties. There was just fear, because we'd heard the Messerschmitts and the ground rumbling around us.

As we passed through Orel I saw another sight I'll never forget; the train ahead of us had been bombed and the station was burning. As we passed the station I remember that I could feel the heat from the flames, as if they were right in our boxcar. I could see human bodies scattered amid the destroyed train cars. It's impossible for me to forget any of this.

We stopped for a long time in Moscow. The first snow had already fallen. Our train was set to go to a factory, and they knew there would be people in several of the boxcars. We stood waiting beside a *burzhuika*, which warmed us some.[1]

The train took us to the Ural mountains area, in Siberia, to a small town in the Kemerovo region (I don't recall the name). At that time in the Soviet Union people would say, "He who doesn't work doesn't eat," so with two children to feed my mother found work quite fast. She received ration cards for bread, sugar, meat, and some type of grain. I remember that when my sister or I lost a ration card it was very dramatic.

Our mother worked in a factory (she was, in general, quite unhealthy and had heart problems) and would return from work very tired with pot of soup that had a spoon attached to it. Aside from this, we had to use ration cards for food. Of course we were hungry, but soon after my father found us via Buguruslan[2]. Before I came to America I went to that same center to pick up documents related to the evacuation. While I was there I was shown a piece of light green paper with my father's handwriting on it. It was his request to find us.

My father wound up in Gorky, 600 kilometers north of Moscow. He picked us up and took us to live with him there. Prior to the war, the

---

[1] A *burzhuika* is a small, rudimentary stove. The word comes from the Russian for bourgeois, *burzhua*.
[2] The Soviet Central Information Office was established in Buguruslan to track evacuees during WWII.

factory in Gorky where he worked built bicycles. Once the war began, the factory started building military motorcycles with sidecars. My father was likely taken there on one of the trains from Kharkov.

The government had forced homeowners to provide rooms for evacuees, so we were given the upper room of a house with five windows. The room wasn't used in winter since it only had a partial wall for the *pechka*, which was in another room.[3] The winter of 1941-1942 was so cold that we didn't go to school. We didn't even have winter clothes. I remember that a glass of water on our table froze in that room.

My sister and I would sit by the wall of the *pechka*, across from the windows, and rub against the wall for heat. We did this so much that in the spring we could see the fire inside the *pechka*, through the wall. We were very cold and very hungry, and I became ill. I had horrible headaches, and could not look directly into lights. My family would cover the lamps for me. Since that time I never use overhead lights; just one or two lamps, and I've suffered from headaches ever since as well.

We felt better with our father near us. Both of my parents worked, but my father worked a lot. He was a barber before the war and had soft hands, but during the war he worked as a grinder Gorky, and was a real workaholic, sometimes working more than 16 hours in a day. They considered him a Stakhanovite.[4] My mother would sell any awards he received (during the war they gave wine and vodka as awards instead of money).

We were given a ramshackle home to live in with a dirt floor. This time we lived by ourselves. Three-fourths of the room was taken up with a large Russian *pechka*, which we would lay on and watch our mother give bottles of wine and vodka to large men who gave her money in return for them. The next day she would go to the market and buy bread.

I didn't start school until after the New Year because I was sick. The factory issued my father size 10 boots with canvas tops, and even though I was a little girl I wore those boots to school. The school closer to our

---

[3] A *pechka* was an oven that doubled as a furnace. In many cases people could sleep on them to keep warm in winter as well.

[4] A very hard worker. The Soviet term comes from Aleksey Stakhanov, who reportedly mined 102 tons of coal in less than six hours (14 times his quota) in 1935.

house had been converted into a hospital, so we had to walk five kilometers to a different school. The second school was so filled with students that we had to attend in shifts, which meant we returned home late each night. During a bombing one day, they made us go outside, and somehow I ended up in a snowdrift. I couldn't get out and wound up with frostbite on my legs and arms. Now I'm very happy to be in Tucson, since all my life in Kharkov I had to buy special mittens to keep my hands warm in winter. Even now I often have cold hands, but that's all trivial, the trivialities of the war years.

There were several military factories in Gorky, and when the Germans approached Moscow they started bombing those factories. We didn't live near the aviation and automobile factories that were making tanks and other combat equipment, but we could see the fires off in the distance.

Kharkov was liberated on August 23, 1943. My mother began to gather our things for the trip home, which we finally made in the summer of 1944. The factory wouldn't release my father because we were still at war.

The three of us (my mother, sister and I) returned to Kharkov. Once we arrived, we found a huge crater where our house used to be. It had been a beautiful apartment building, two stories with stained glass windows.

Relatives of ours, who'd arrived earlier, provided us with shelter. They lived with other families in one large room, and we slept on the floor until we could get our own room. My mother's older sister had been a doctor at the front, and she began the process of getting us an *attestat*, since we were considered family of a service member at the front.[5] Because of this we received a room in an apartment with five other families. There was one toilet for everyone, and one wash basin in the kitchen. It had a cook top in the kitchen that didn't work because there was no gas. Each room had its own *pechka* stoked with wood. This is where we cooked our food.

The war ended, but the factory in Gorky still wouldn't release my father. In late 1947 he fell ill with malaria, and my mother went to take

---

[5] *Attestat* was a certificate issued to support families of officers who had served in the Red Army. It made certain allowances available to families, including cash.

care of him. Only then would they let him return to his family. My father had the highest qualifications as a grinder, and was involved in making motorcycle part number 226. He was one of the only grinders who could make that part. He was a workaholic.

My father's malaria cleared up quickly after he returned to Kharkov. It's possible the change in climate helped him, but he remained quite weak and didn't work for some time after. He eventually went to work as a barber.

I graduated from school in 1948 and was accepted to attend university, where I studied biology. The competition was fierce, but I was accepted. I wanted to be a doctor, and was later accepted to study animal and human physiology. This allowed me to attend postgraduate medical school after I graduated and worked some. I was already married by the time I graduated from the institute in 1953.

Although I was an active, excellent student, I was unable to find work right away because my passport showed that I was Jewish.[6] Specialists were needed everywhere, but once I showed my passport people would apologize and claim the positions were taken. This occurred many times.

This went on until 1955, when I'd already had my daughter. One of my classmates introduced me to the director of the pathology laboratory at an ophthalmic institute. I became a laboratory technician at the scientific research center at Girshman Medical Institute. Professor Kopid taught me a lot related to pathology while I was there.

I took time off from work and began a two-year postgraduate medical school program, then returned to the laboratory. When Professor Kopid retired I became head of the laboratory. I was a junior researcher and was working on my dissertation when all of the scientific research centers in Kharkov were closed in 1963. Their closures echoed the "Doctor's Plot," as all of the branch chiefs in the ophthalmic institute were Jews who'd been in the war and had received awards.[7] They were all highly

---

[6] Block Five of the Soviet passport indicated nationality. Soviet Jews were required to use "Jewish" in the nationality block.

[7] In 1952 a group of prominent Moscow doctors, primarily Jewish, was accused of conspiring to kill Soviet leaders. This "Doctor's Plot" led to the dismissal or arrest of numerous doctors nationwide. Krushchev denounced the conspiracy in 1955.

intelligent PhD candidates, and I was lucky to have worked 10 years with them.

Our institute was closed. I began working at a regional health station, in charge of the food hygiene laboratory, where I worked for 30 years. I resigned from work two weeks before I left for the United States. I was involved in studies related to the influence of microwaves on B vitamins, and I've had several articles published on nutrition. I arrived in Tucson in January 1996.

Paulina Goldberg

Ukraine

It is 2011 and I am now eighty-two years old. While it's awful to have to say that, I don't feel the heavy load of previous years, even though there was the war (1941 to 1945) and my immigration. I have promised to keep our family tree for the next generation, which is dedicated to the blessed memory of our ancestors.

My great-grandmother's name was Sura, and my great-grandfather was Isaak Lorkis. They were born in Ukraine in the 19th century. They had five children: three daughters (Berta, Fira and Basya), and two sons (Aron and Isay).

Berta was my grandmother, so I will begin with a description of her and my grandfather, Pinkhus Povolotsky. My grandfather never got to see me, as he died in January of 1929 and I was born that March. My mother said he was very kind, sympathetic, cheerful and beautiful. He loved music, played the violin, and worked in a sugar factory in the city of Cherkassy, Ukraine. My grandmother Berta was a housewife and raised the children. They lived modestly, and my grandmother dressed modestly but nicely and looked wonderful even when she was older. She had a beautiful figure and I always admired her. She died in Cherkassy at the age of 93 (in 1969), out-living my grandfather by 40 years.

My grandparents had four children: Klara (my mother), Busya, Lenya and Frida. They were very happy, and despite the fact that they lived in various cities (Moscow, Dnepropetrovsk and Cherkassy) their relationship was close, even though in those days there were no cell phones. Mostly they communicated through letters. Telephones were only at the main post offices, where there were telephone booths. Sometimes we had to make reservations to talk, waiting many hours for the operator to connect us.

Klara met the handsome Yakov Goldberg, and in 1921 they married. Klara and Yakov had two daughters: my older sister Inna (born in 1923) and me (born in 1929). Our childhood was extremely difficult because of World War II, which occurred in the Soviet Union from 1941 to 1945.

From 1936 through 1941 (prior to the war), we lived in Dnepropetrovsk, and on the first day of the war the Nazis bombed the city. Wounded soldiers were soon coming to the city and were placed in schools converted into hospitals. My mother and I cared for the wounded, but not for long because two months later – in August 1941 – the fascists were already at the city's outskirts. My father was drafted into the army, while my mother, my sister and I tried to run from the city. We went to the railroad station and rode in boxcars crammed with so many people that we could only stand up. The trains headed east, away from Ukraine. We ran without having time to take any necessities and without a single *kopek*, but we were young and bravely endured the hunger, cold and heat.[1] Low-flying enemy aircraft bombed the trains, and many people perished along the way. It's a true miracle that we survived. The Germans were overtaking us, getting closer and closer, and we went farther and farther to the east.

Our first stop was a village in the Krasnodar region, and then in the North Caucasus – the city of Ordzhonikidze (now called Vladikavkaz). For several months I attended the sixth grade there, but when the Germans approached the city we had to move again, first to Nalchik, then to Mineralnye Vody and Pyatigorsk. It was there, on Mashuk Mountain, where we came face-to-face with German forces on motorcycles. Miraculously, one of our military vehicles picked us up and we passed by the Germans. Standing in the back of the truck, we endured the Georgian Military Road and arrived in Gori (Stalin's birthplace), where we were immediately bombed.[2] Barely surviving, we knew we had to move on. Our goal was to get to the town in the Ural mountains where aunt from Dnepropetrovsk had gone. It seemed to us that if we could get there we'd be safe. But it was not to be: the road to the Urals became a six-month ordeal.

---

[1] A *kopek* is one-hundredth of the Russian Ruble.
[2] The Georgian Military Road runs through the Caucusus from Georgia to Russia.

At that time it was impossible to cross the Caspian Sea. Tens of thousand of people were at the large pier in Baku, living for months under the hot sun and infested with lice, waiting to cross. We were among them. When we finally did, we found ourselves in Central Asia. We were constantly hungry, dirty, and without proper clothing. Some locals brought food, water and clothes to the railroad station and distributed it to people. We reached the Urals in time to endure the cruel winter of 1941-1942.

We stopped at the Novo-Sergeevka railroad station in Orenburg region, where an elderly local woman took us in. There was a *pechka* (known as a *burzhuika*) in our small room.[3] Our room was heated with dried cow dung which we collected on village roads. We slept on hay and ate soup made from potato peels or bran, and in the summer we lived on nature's gifts. Soon, Inna began working in a factory and we were a little better off. Workers were given food cards for 400 grams of bread a day, and 200 grams for every dependent. We were no longer so hungry, and that's how we lived until 1943.

Having saved money for a ticket, Inna went to Grandmother Berta's home in Moscow to study, as she had finished her first year at Dnepropetrovsk Metallurgy Institute prior to the war. Inna graduated from the Moscow Nonferrous Metals and Gold Institute in 1947. She was assigned as a junior research associate at the Scientific Research Institute, then as shift supervisor in a Moscow factory.

After Inna went to Moscow, my mother and I went as well. We didn't have enough money to go all the way, and I recall that we rode on a train loaded with coal. When we got off the train at Ramenskoe station, near Moscow, we had to clean ourselves as best we could at a water fountain because we were covered in coal dust. We arrived in Moscow relatively "clean." There were five of us living with our Grandmother Berta and our Aunt Busya (my mother's sister) in a 16-square-meter room in a communal apartment, where nine other families lived.[1] There was one toilet and one bath for the 45 people living in the commune.

---

[3] A *pechka* was an oven that doubled as a furnace. In many cases people could sleep on them to keep warm in winter as well. A *burzhuika* was a small, rudimentary stove. The word comes from the Russian for bourgeois, *burzhua*.
[1] 16-square meters is slightly over 172-square feet.

In 1944 we tracked down my father (his military unit was located in Rostov-on-Don) and reunited with him. In 1945, when he was demobilized, we returned to Dnepropetrovsk. I finished the ninth and tenth grades in Rostov-on-Don, and in 1946 I attended Dnepropetrovsk University to study chemistry, which I completed in 1951. That same year I married Mikhail Gorbakovskiy, who was nine years older than me and had been in World War II. He was 21 when the war began, and had completed his third year at the railroad institute in Dnepropetrovsk. On June 22, 1941, the students took their final examinations and were immediately mobilized. By the end of June, they were sent to dig foxholes and trenches, to build bunkers, and to install barbed wire at the city's outskirts. This meant the students were at frontal locations practically unarmed. They were given some rifles and helmets, but hardly anyone had them. Like many students, it was the first time Mikhail had held a rifle. None of the students thought of themselves – they fought to the death defending the city.

Enveloped in smoke and flames, the city fiercely resisted. The fight was for every factory, every street, and every home. Out of the 900 students in his group, Mikhail was among only 70 who survived. For his bravery and courage, Mikhail was awarded the "Order of the Patriotic War" and a variety of other medals.

Mikhail graduated from the Transport Institute and worked as an engineer in a diesel locomotive factory. Beginning in 1956, he started teaching at an Industrial College, which he did for 25 years. For his many years of hard work, high professionalism, and for teaching young professionals, he was awarded the title "Veteran of Labor." Mikhail died in Tucson, Arizona, in 1999.

I graduated in chemistry from the University in 1951. 1951-1952 were peak years of anti-Semitism, when the Soviets tried the Kremlin's Jewish doctors (later rehabilitated) as enemies of the people[5]. I remember that when I was in my fifth year at the institute we had a meeting concerning two Jewish teachers, Kolbovsky and Shukhman. Their good

---

[5] In 1952 a group of prominent Moscow doctors, primarily Jewish, was accused of conspiring to kill Soviet leaders. This "Doctor's Plot" led to the dismissal or arrest of numerous doctors nationwide. Krushchev denounced the conspiracy in 1955.

names were disgraced because they had supposedly remained behind in Tashkent during the war and didn't defend their homeland. It was decided that there was no place for them at the institute. They were thrown out of the party, and, naturally, couldn't remain as teachers.

I started searching for a job after I received my diploma, but finding work was virtually impossible. I was refused work, under various pretexts, once those doing the hiring saw my passport.[6]

While at the University, the Komsomol district committee knew that I was a good activist.[7] They called a metallurgic factory and recommended me for work there, which helped me get the job. I started as a laboratory assistant, and mastered spectral-analysis. I was later asked to work at the Metallurgic Institute, where I remained for 33 years. In 1967 I defended my dissertation and was promoted to Senior Research Associate.

Many years later, in 1969, when our son Edward submitted his application to the Dnepropetrovsk Institute of Metallurgy, they wouldn't accept his documents because there was a checkmark next to his name. This meant he had been blacklisted. It turned out that the admissions committee realized they had a large shortfall in the chemistry department, only seven people for 30 seats. Edward gave them his documents, took the entrance examinations (with excellent marks), and was enrolled for his first year. After completing that year with honors, he went to the head of the institute to request a transfer into the steel-casting department.

After graduation, my son married and worked at the Ferrous Metals Scientific Research Institute in Donetsk. He defended his dissertation and received his PhD. However, following the collapse of the Soviet Union in 1991 – 1992, work at the institute was scaled back, and people lost their jobs. Edward and his family (his wife and her parents) decided to leave Ukraine. My sister, husband and I were left alone, and since we only had one son we decided to join him. Two years later we did just that.

Thank you, America, for the warm reception, and for giving us the ability to live in a place that cares for us.

---

[6] Block Five of the Soviet passport indicated nationality. Soviet Jews were required to use "Jewish" in this nationality block.

[7] Komsomol was the youth division of the Communist Party in the Soviet Union.

Wolfgang Hellpap

Germany

I was born in Berlin, Germany, on June 25, 1931, the only child of Max Hirschel, a Polish man in textile sales, and Klara Hellpap, a pediatric nurse. My father was Jewish and my mother was Christian. My father would visit us from time to time, but I don't know much about his family. He left Berlin before everything started. My parents never married.

The first experience I had with anti-Semitism in Germany was in 1937, when I went to school. According to the Nuremberg laws, Jewish children couldn't attend school, but my mother somehow got me into one. I made it to the second grade before they found out I was officially Jewish. They kicked me out of school in the middle of class, when the teacher said she had my name on a list and told me to leave. That was the law. All of a sudden the other kids were throwing rocks and spitting at me, so I had to run as fast as I could. I was crying.

My mother wanted to keep me where she lived, but she couldn't. She had just one room in another person's apartment, and the owner wouldn't allow me to be there. She wanted to ask her relatives to hide me, but the German police insisted I wear the Star of David and report in every two weeks at the precinct. In the meantime, my problem was finding a place to stay.

I looked for places, even though I was only seven- or eight-years old. Most of the time I'd stay with family, but they'd only let me stay a few nights at a time, and then I'd have to hide elsewhere, sometimes in old sheds in the parks. I was so young that I thought there must be something awfully wrong with me. I was afraid of the police, and would try to hide the Star of David. My mother had to work and couldn't have me in her apartment. She'd say that someone would eventually tell the Gestapo, so I had to stay at various places temporarily.

The police finally found me when I was staying with one of my relatives and decided to go out. They put me in a Jewish orphanage – just a little camp really – where even some of the Jewish teachers cooperated with the authorities. It was an awful place, but it got worse once the Germans started transporting some of the kids to camps. The Gestapo would usually come at night with a list of names, and the teacher really liked it. He had a whip, and every time the Gestapo called out a name the teacher would crack that whip right at the child, in bed. Imagine being nine-years old, hoping they didn't call your name.

In 1940 my mother was finally able to get me out of the orphanage. She went to the Gestapo and argued that I wasn't actually Jewish and shouldn't be persecuted. They told her I could stay with her, but I'd still have to report to them every two weeks. She was working as a telephone operator then, and she was so afraid. When we'd go out I had to wear the Star of David, but my mother was a Christian.

I had an uncle who lived outside Berlin, and he agreed to hide me. He said I'd have to live in the shed that hid the water meter and not in the house. I had stopped reporting to the police, so they put out a warrant for me. I was officially in a kind of parolee status – and I'd violated my parole.

The years went by, and then the allied bombing began. This was in 1943, when I was twelve years old. At that point I was living with my mother again, but when the bombing started I wasn't allowed to go into the cellar where everyone else was hiding. I had to stay upstairs instead, where I watched the buildings fall after the bombs fell. These bombings went on day and night, yet I wasn't allowed in the shelter. I survived by the grace of G-d.

I had to teach myself a lot of things, like how to read and write. I found out that the war had ended by reading the papers. The Russians started moving into Berlin, so the streets were mayhem. There were rumors they wanted to flood the whole city. The day I realized it was over we were in a basement, and when we looked out we saw a Russian tank there. We debated who should go out to look. My uncle said I should go, and show them my Star of David. So I did.

A Russian officer near the tank saw my Star of David and started yelling happily at me in Russian. I was so excited. He came to me and said, "*khleb?*" meaning "do you want some bread?" I told him, "Yes!" The Russians had already liberated many camps by then, so they knew.

The Jewish organizations started looking for survivors, especially the HIAS.[1] They found me finally, and told me I was going to Israel, which at the time was Palestine. They organized a bus, and I left with another 10 or so Jewish children. I said goodbye to my mother and told her I hoped that I could bring her to Palestine later.

The bus took us from Germany to France. Each time we'd pass the Russians they'd yell, "Go to Moscow!" We stayed near Paris, where we were told we would go to Israel on a ship from Marseilles once the English agreed that we could. When they finally did, we went to Marseilles, where we had to wait another two months. We finally boarded a ship and sailed to Israel, where we were the first Jewish children to make *aliyah* to Tel Aviv.[2]

There was a well-known woman in Israel named Hannah Chizhik who founded a large compound in the middle of Tel Aviv to teach children. I was almost fourteen years old by then, and I was finally catching up on my schooling. We were isolated for awhile in 1946 because of a bubonic plague outbreak in Palestine. The British would shoot people right in the streets if they thought they had the plague.

I was able to get my mother to Palestine in 1947, and we were sent to a special *kibbutz* for German Jews. One unfortunate problem was that the people on the *kibbutz* no longer wished to speak German, which is all my mother could speak. So it was difficult for her.

The State of Israel was formed in 1948, and right away the surrounding Arab countries wanted war with the new state. A friend and I decided we wanted to fight. There wasn't a real army yet, but there were these different factions, like *Haganah*.[3] We went to basic training, and in the meantime eight Arab countries came at Israel from all sides. Ironically, the rifles we were learning to fire were German made.

---

[1] The Hebrew Immigrant Aid Society.
[2] *Aliyah*, defined from Hebrew as "ascent" or "going up," is a basic tenet of Zionism and was the post-World War II term for mass immigration of Jews to Israel.
[3] Haganah was a Jewish paramilitary organization in what was then the British Mandate of Palestine from 1920-1948.

One day they told us an Iraqi Army group was coming, so we went into battle for the first time. Iraqis were known for being cowardly, and we shot as much as we could until they ran. The Marines took over for us, and after boot camp my friend and I were sent to Jerusalem.

A very well equipped, really good Jordanian faction was in Jerusalem, coached and supported by the British. They were trying to chase all of us out of Jerusalem. During one of the fights, my friend and I were running across a field and I was shot in the leg. We made it to a field hospital, where it was complete mayhem. The doctor looked at my leg and said, "Cut it off." My friend, Peter, pointed his gun at the doctor and said, "You take off his leg, I shoot. I'll pull this trigger." So the doctor told them to put me in a bed. I was there for a few months, and then they sent me back into combat.

We fought the Egyptians in the Negev.[1] They weren't as good as the Jordanians, and would often run. Sometimes we'd even put props up, fake artillery and things like that, and they'd still run. We wound up taking prisoners, and because I was just seventeen years old they told me I'd be one of the people accompanying them. When I did I heard some of the prisoners speaking German, and reported that to my superiors. There were eight Arab nations fighting us, and now there were even Germans. They weren't treated very well – they were killed.

I had to start earning a living, so I started in air conditioning. I learned a lot about electricity and such things in Tel Aviv. My mother and I never really made much headway in Israel, so she suggested we go to America. But there were no visas available, so in 1953 we decided to go back to Germany.

We arrived in Stuttgart, Germany, with little money, and tried to find relatives. Once again I went to HIAS to tell them I wanted to go to America. They checked me out to make sure I was Jewish, and agreed to help. My mother and I left for America in 1955, and in 1956 I got drafted in the U.S. Army, in San Francisco, so I had to go to basic training again.

The U.S. Army shipped me back to Germany, this time as an American soldier. The army stationed me in Stuttgart, so my friends that

---

[1] The Negev is a mostly desert region in southern Israel.

still lived there didn't believe I'd even left. I was in the army for two years and returned to San Francisco after. I worked as an industrial lab technician, but eventually started my own janitorial business. I moved to Arizona in 2005 to retire.

I have three sons who know about my ordeals. I want them to remember me as someone who went through many travails and still succeeded. I want them to remember to never give up.

Czechoslovakia/Hungary

I was born on May 2, 1933, in the Carpathian area of Czechoslovakia, in the village of Nadbereg.[1] My parents divorced when I was young, and my father lived in America, in New York. My mother married a second time to an accountant, a very good man. They worked very hard at raising us, and then we were sent to Auschwitz.

Prior to 1939 our region was occupied by the Czechoslovakian Army, but in 1939 the Hungarian Army arrived and took over. At that point we were considered to be in Hungary. There was still some peace, but not like there had been during the Czech period. Under Czechoslovakian rule life was wonderful. By 1943 the conditions had turned very poor, especially for Jews.

In 1944 the Germans finally arrived. They were in Hungary prior to that, in Budapest, but not near us. Once they arrived in our area they began taking us away to the camps. They didn't take us all at once, but put us first in a ghetto in Beregovo, a city near our village, and then took us in groups to Auschwitz. They took my step-father, mother, sister and me at the same time. My mother's father had died in 1935, but my grandmother was still alive. She was living at the time with another one of her daughters in the Beregovo ghetto.

They took us to a train station and put us into boxcars made for horses and other animals. Right after we arrived at the camp, a man yelled in Hungarian: "twins, doctors, and pharmacists!" My sister and I were twins, but we stood there with our mother. They took the three of us away and tattooed us, gave us numbers on our arms. After 70 years,

---

[1] The borders of Hungary, Poland, Ukraine, and the former Czechoslovakia were redrawn prior to and after the war. Ms. Himmel's first language is Hungarian.

my number hasn't faded. They found a place for our mother in a labor camp, and we were in that camp as well but in the children's block, where they kept the twins.[2]

There were around 200 to 250 pairs of twins in the camp. Doctor Mengele was there, and conducted experiments on twins. Every three or four weeks they would take blood from us for some type of experiment. We didn't eat well, but we were in the worker's camp so we ate better than some. That was important, since they tested our blood and checked our eyes, hair, height and weight.

They had adult twins there as well. I remember there were two adult twins from Holland, Helga and her sister, whose name I can't remember. We only talked with the children who spoke Hungarian, like us, and not with the children who spoke other languages. We'd always spoken Hungarian in our home, even though my village was in Czechoslovakia when I was born.

I don't want to remember the camp. It was horrible. The children's block was right next to the block where they took the dead and dying from the labor camp. There were so many dead bodies, all naked. It was horrible to see: young people, the elderly, and children. I will never forget it – I would like to forget, but I can't. We could have gone outside the barracks, but the building with the dead and dying was right there. We didn't want to go outside.

My sister and I were able to secretly communicate with our mother when she was in the labor camp at Auschwitz, but in September 1944 they took her to Germany with other laborers. She survived and returned home after the liberation, but her legs were in bad condition. My poor step-father died in another camp after it was liberated. He was also taken to Germany, to a labor camp where they needed extra workers. The work there was difficult, as it was in a missile factory.

We twins weren't required to do anything in the camp. Perhaps other children worked; we didn't know. But the twins did nothing. They did take us once to harvest tomatoes in a garden. In general we didn't do anything. We ate, but not properly. There was a set of triplets, two boys and a girl, and only one of the boys lived. The other two died because

---

[2] Ms. Himmel and her twin sister (and their mother) were sent from the main camp at Auschwitz to Birkenau labor camp.

there wasn't enough food. Some died even after the Russians liberated us. The Russians didn't give us anything to eat either.

We didn't have proper beds in the barracks we lived in, just wooden planks without mattresses. We had things to cover up with, but it was not like home. It was very cold. The last time the Germans took us anywhere was in December 1944. They were leaving by then, because the Russian Army was very close. At first the Germans left, but then they returned to take those of us that remained at Birkenau back to Auschwitz. Strangely, though we were children, we were taken after the adults. When we arrived at Auschwitz, we saw that the adults just standing there, not moving. We wondered what had happened.

The Germans escaped and left us at the side of the road. There were nice buildings not far away, so we went there. A woman from our village was there with her daughter, who was two years older than my sister and me. The daughter had survived well, and had been put to work. They'd found the place where the Germans cooked, and there was still a little food left, so the woman started cooking what she could: potatoes and potato soup. We took the soup to another building where other people were staying. There were only men there, all of them bare-boned. We were eleven years old then, and found our uncle in that building, which was truly a miracle. Every day we brought him food and fed him.

We stayed there for a while, because there was nowhere else to go. Everything around us was bombed. Finally, either in January or February, they took the children to Katowice, in Poland. There were French people in Katowice who would say to us, "Come to France with us, you can live with us. We will be your parents." But we didn't want to.

We couldn't get home because all the routes were bombed and the trains couldn't move. In March the Russians assigned a soldier to us, and we were put into boxcars, the same sort that we'd arrived in. The Russian escorted us home. We knew how to get home because we'd talked with our parents about this. We had even determined where we'd meet them.

When we arrived home none of our family members were there. We lived with strangers in our village, which was then controlled by the Russians. Finally, others started coming home. My uncle arrived first, my mother's brother, then my mother's sister arrived, my aunt. She was the one my grandmother had lived with. It turned out that my grandmother had been taken to Auschwitz with my aunt. They kept my aunt to work in the labor camp and killed my grandmother. This was how things were in the camp: the old were led to the gas chambers and the young were taken away to be used as labor. I remember that when we arrived at the camp someone pointed at the tall smoke stacks, the sorts you see at factories, and said, "See that? That's where your grandmother is now."

My aunt had a wonderful family before the war: a good husband and two sons. The older son was sixteen and the younger son was the same age as my sister and me. Except for my aunt, the rest of them died in the camps. After everyone else had returned home, my mother arrived. She had survived.

Afterwards, there were people in Hungary who would say, "You came home better off than when you left," but there are just those sorts of people. How can people be so bad? But there were also very wonderful people who I will never forget. When we were still in the ghetto, one of our village neighbors baked bread and brought it to us there. She risked her life doing that, because she could have been forced to remain with us. She wasn't Jewish; she was a Jehovah's Witness. She was a wonderful woman. There were no neighbors like that in the camps. Nobody even cared for the children there.

We left for Israel in 1972, where we lived for three years. Then my husband went to America, where his cousins lived. They were his age and had invited him to come. My husband went a little earlier than the rest of the family to find work. We all arrived in America in 1975. My real father, who had moved to America when I was very young, died in 1969, so I never got to see him. But he would send packages to us in our village after Hungary was under Russian control.

The tattoo on my arm still shows. It is A-3638. My sister's was A-3637, and my mother's was A-3636. They gave us these numbers in order, and when they called my sister and me for our blood tests they didn't use our names; they called out our numbers. In Auschwitz, our numbers were our names.

Liza Iakover

Ukraine

I was born on November 6, 1923, in Odessa, Ukraine.[1] My mother, Dvoyra Moiseyevna, was a housewife and sewed very well. She was born in Odessa and had two sisters and two brothers. Her older brother, Gersh, was mobilized in World War I and went to the front, where he was captured. After the war he lived in Brussels, Belgium. He was found dead in his home in 1932, though there are few details about how he died. My mother's sister, Yevgeniya, was a doctor and was mobilized in the Great Patriotic War.[2] She was killed in Borisov. My mother's brother, Boris, went to Palestine in the 1920s and her sister Khaya evacuated to Tashkent during the war.

My father, Sanya Abramovich Iakover, was a clothing salesman. During Lenin's New Economic Policy he opened a small clothing shop, but after two years he went bankrupt.[3] Nevertheless, the Soviet government considered him unemployed, and because of that our family was evicted from our apartment in 1930. After some time, my father found work in a store, but they fired him. Our family lived with friends, and then settled in the village of Chubayevka, Ukraine. My father had three brothers: one was killed in the civil war, another was killed in World War II, and the third went to Palestine in the 1920s.

My eldest sister Fira went to school, but after the seventh grade she had to go to FZU, because my father was unemployed.[4] She later took courses to get into an institute, and graduated from the Pharmaceutical

---

[1] Liza is the sister of another author in this series, Rakhil Yakover.
[2] "Great Patriotic War" is the term most often used for World War II in the former Soviet Union. It is still in use today.
[3] The New Economic Policy temporarily authorized citizens to own businesses.
[4] FZU was factory-based vocational schooling.

Institute and post-graduate school. When the war began she was mobilized to work in a laboratory that made mortar shells. Although she was a pharmacist, the authorities directed her to work where she was needed. She was evacuated along with the rest of the institute to Tashkent, where she worked as a pharmacist, and received notification there that her husband had been killed in the war. Fira remarried after the war and had two children.

I started school in 1931. In all of Odessa, there were just two schools that taught in Russian and two that taught in Yiddish. The rest taught in the Ukrainian language. I went to a Ukrainian school, because it was closer to our house. Three years later, Skripnik committed suicide and the schools began translating their courses into Russian.[5] However, I stayed in the Ukrainian school. I went from class-to-class with certificates of excellence, and graduated with an honors diploma. On June 19, 1941, we had our graduation ceremony and party, and we made plans for our futures. I was prepared to apply to a technical institute, but on June 22 the war began.

That day I heard my sister Fira cry out after hearing over the radio that the war had begun. She was frightened because her husband was in the Army and was stationed on the Romanian border (he was killed in 1943 at Kerch). A month later, the Germans began bombing Odessa. I went to Proletarsky Boulevard Station in September 1941, to dig foxholes, and on September 9, 1941, the Germans bombed Odessa all night long. The next morning my father came to see if I was alive or not.

Why didn't we evacuate like so many others did? Because my father believed that the Germans wouldn't do anything bad to us. He said that the Germans were a very cultured people. Later, when we were in the ghetto, I asked my father the same question many times: "How is it that you're such a wise man, and many people come to you for advice, but you believe the Germans?"

On October 16, 1941, the Germans and Romanians entered Odessa, and on October 22 partisans blew up the Romanian headquarters building. The next day, all down Shevchenko Avenue, there were dead bodies piled up, and people hanging. Within days, a declaration was

---

[5] Nikolay Skripnik was a Ukrainian Bolshevik and a proponent of Ukrainian independence. Blocked by the Soviets, he committed suicide prior to being tried.

hung on each of our gates announcing that all Jewish people had to appear for registration at Dalnik, an area in Odessa. Along the way we were taken to a prison, where we stayed for 10 days. They released us after the anniversary of the October Revolution celebrations in Moscow. Just outside the prison we came across a pile of dead bodies.

The order came in January 1942 for all Jewish people to be transferred to Slobodka (an area in Odessa) and live with residents there.[6] The winter of 1941-1942 was very cold, and there were many frozen bodies in the streets. People were freezing to death or dying of hunger.

In February the Nazis began removing the Jews from Odessa. On February 9, 1942, they loaded us on a freight train so full that I couldn't breathe: I had one foot on the floor and the other up in the air. They took us to Mostovaya station, and from there we walked to Domanevka.[7] Along the way we came across frozen bodies and others who'd been executed. There was a man walking with us blinded with his own tears because he'd been forced to kill his friends. We walked for about two weeks.

My mother, father, younger sister Rakhil, and I were housed in barracks at Domanevka. All of Domanevka's previous prisoners had been sent to Bogdanovka, where almost 60,000 Jews were burned to death.[8] We were the first to stay in Domanevka after that. The leader there was Leleka, who treated Jews with respect and allowed those with a trade to live with peasants there. Because my mother could sew we were allowed to live in a peasant's house. She sewed various items so she could work for a little money.

A typhoid epidemic began in the spring, though now it's said that we were purposefully infected. My mother, my sister Rakhil, and I all fell ill. My father had typhoid earlier, in 1921. After Leleka died from typhoid, the police chased all of the Jewish people from the peasant homes back into the Domanevka barracks.

---

[6] Slobodka was a ghetto established in Odessa.

[7] Approximately 8,000 Jews were held at Domanevka, a concentration camp run primarily by Romanian forces.

[8] Bogdanovka was a ghetto. Romanian troops and Ukrainian auxiliaries massacred almost all of the approximately 54,000 Jews there in December, 1941.

My mother died from typhoid on May 1, 1942. Her body was put on the *pechka*, and the police came five times that day to take us to the barracks.[9] My father wasn't with us in the hut, as he had gone to a friend's house, so the police told the peasant we were staying with: "We'll come back tonight to execute everyone, and we demand that you get rid of the bodies." That night we removed my mother's body (during the day a special brigade went through the village gathering up bodies for a common gravesite), and hid it in the woodshed between the cows. In the morning, we were taken to the barracks. A policeman on horseback pushed my father and me along.

After several days they took us to Akhmechetka concentration camp, on the banks of the Bug River.[10] People could see dirt moving in common graves, because the people buried there were still alive. At Akhmechetka they put us in the pig pens on an old pig farm.

The police would escort people from Akhmechetka to the village for water. On one of these trips, a young policeman exchanged pleasantries with a girl, saying: "I'm going to shoot a bird now." He shot one person in the leg, and another in the arm. Another time, a policeman beat my father because he'd swapped my winter coat with a peasant instead of him.

They eventually started assigning Jews to collective farms. All of the men had been mobilized, so there was no one left to work the fields. Women had to leave their small children behind to go to these farms. Around 25 people, including my father, sister, and me, were sent to the Koshtov collective farm to work. We lived in rat-infested sheds there, and slept on beds made of wormwood to keep away the fleas. A peasant woman baked bread for us, complaining that she couldn't knead the dough enough to bake it because it contained flour from oats, millet, and barley. She added potatoes and pumpkin to make the flour sticky.

We worked the vegetable gardens in the fields, and in the fall we harvested reeds in the marshes, which we used to make blankets and to cover our roofs. We walked barefoot in the swampy areas, and leaches

---

[9] A *pechka* is a type of stove unit that includes a fireplace, cooking area, and a bed above it that's heated from the stove.

[10] Approximately 18,000 Jews were held at Akhmetchetka, a concentration camp run primarily by Romanian forces.

attached to our legs. We sat down to rest in a field one day, but a Romanian guard ordered us to get up and work. We told him we were tired and would rest a bit, then work. The next day he brought soldiers who beat us up because the Romanian had told them we were talking about Stalin.

We soaked and dried hemp in the winter, which we used to make thread and cloth, then sacks from the cloth. We harvested corn, which chaffed the skin on our fingers. There was no way to heal the chaffing wounds.

My father took care of the horses. Two horses ran off one day, and a policeman beat my father even though he knew the horses would return. My father got frostbite on his legs that winter, which turned into gangrene. He died on December 16, 1943. The ground was frozen, so the men could only dig a shallow grave next to the road. In the spring, water washed my father's body up, and we had to rebury him.

A year later they transferred us back to Akhmechetka to dig anti-tank ditches near the Bug River. We lived in a little hut and dried hemp in that same area. One day a man drying hemp fell asleep and a spark from the stove started a fire. We ran out in the snow while our hut burned. I wound up with painful blisters and couldn't sit or lie down. We had no medications, so I treated myself with a hot brick. I was ready to cut my wrists from the pain, but I decided I wanted to live to see victory.

In the spring of 1944 we began hearing battles nearby and decided to return to the farm at Koshtov. The peasants there knew us, so we were confident they would hide us. On March 28, 1944, several men showed up at the farm to liberate us. Odessa was liberated on April 10, 1944, and on April 16 we returned to the city. We got there by walking, though part of the way we rode on a tank. Our apartment was now occupied, but because our parents perished we didn't want to live there anyways. One of our neighbors took us in and gave us a small room, which was fine with us: we were happy to be back in Odessa.

A communist youth organization helped me find a job in the library at the Nautical School, where I worked seven years. I enrolled in the university at the same time, taking chemistry classes through correspondence. After a year the university director decided not to allow correspondence courses in the chemistry department. When I went to him for permission to enroll in day classes, he called his secretary and snapped at her, telling her not to send students in to see him. "I want only Ukrainian students," he said.

I transferred to take correspondence courses in commercial refrigeration in the technology department at the Food Institute. Working and going to school was not easy. I graduated in 1952 and was sent to Leningrad to work in a bread factory as a technologist (it was the first time I'd ever seen a bread factory). I worked at the factory for 33 years (three years as a shift technologist, seven as a shift supervisor, seven as a senior technologist, 16-and-a-half years as the laboratory director).

There were many tests and several incidents at the factory, such as when the department director told me one day, "Go to your Israel!" When the factory director found out about the incident, he told me to make a complaint with the party committee, but I decided I wouldn't do that. Only three of us in the factory were Jewish, and most of the workers treated me well. I worked there until 1986, when my grandson was born, though I was eligible to retire in 1978.

I didn't want to leave the Soviet Union, because when I did I was already old. My daughter and son-in-law insisted I go with them. We departed in 1993. Immigration was a difficult period in my life because of the different languages, cultures, lifestyles, and customs. It's easier for the young than it is the old. I know four languages (Russian, Ukrainian, German, and Yiddish), but that's not enough.[11]

---

[11] Liza Iakover passed away on May 16, 2014.

Lyubov Krimberg

Romania

My name is Lyubov Davidovna Krimberg, maiden name Morgenshtern, born in December 1919, in Kishinev, Moldova. My father fled to France in 1910 because of large pogroms in Kishinev,[1] and worked there as a taxi driver until 1912. My mother went to France and gave birth to my brother, but she grew homesick and returned to Kishinev. When World War I began, my father was in France and my mother was in Moldova.

My father returned to Moldova in 1918, the year before I was born. They were penniless, so my father remained in Kishinev. There wasn't much work available, but because he knew several languages (French, German, and Russian) he was able to work for the French rail company *Wagonlee*.[2] Each international train traveling through Europe had a special sleeping car with bulletproof glass for senior officials, so they needed people who knew many languages. I was five years old when my father was transferred to Bucharest, Romania, where we moved.

I went to school in Romania. When I was fifteen years old I went to ballet school at the Opera Theatre in Bucharest, where I studied for two years. At that time, Europe was already feeling some concern about Hitler's coming to power in Germany, and people were stocking up on salt, sugar, and other products. My brother was living in France, but in 1935 he came to Romania to serve there. Because of the way things had progressed, our parents wanted to send us to Palestine. In 1938 we went

---

[1] A pogrom was an organized massacre of a particular ethnic group, in particular that of Jews in Russia or Eastern Europe.
[2] *Compagnie Internationale des Wagons-Lits* was a company that made train cars, and was particularly known for its on-train catering and sleeping car services.

to Constanta and lived in a hotel, trying to get out of Romania.[3] The Germans invaded Poland in 1939, and the hotel we lived in was surrounded by military members in civilian clothes. They mined the Black Sea at Constanta, but many Jews, wanting to escape, ran to boats and rafts and were killed by the mines in the water. We returned to Bucharest.

In June 1940, the Soviets entered Moldova (it's thought that the Soviet Union freed Moldova, but now it's said they occupied it).[4] The Moldovans were very happy the Russians had come, because Romanians considered Moldovans as third-class people. There were no higher educational institutes in Moldova, and there was no work. The young people went to Romania to work. My father went to the embassy in Bucharest to request approval for us to return to Kishinev, and when it was approved we left with what we had in our suitcases.

My father found work in Moldova as a railroad watchman. In May 1941, my mother became emotionally ill and entered a psychiatric hospital. When my mother was discharged from the hospital, we were told that she had to be kept away from all of the upheaval.

At that time they were making a movie in Moldova called "Bukuria," which translates as "Joy," and they needed dancers. I was selected among the other boys and girls to be in the movie. There were immigrants from many countries: Hungary, Bulgaria, and many more. We danced outside the city and had costumes, fake braids, and rag-like slippers on our feet. On June 22, 1941, I went to the hotel where our film crew was located to receive my first pay of 19 rubles. On my way home, I saw airplanes dropping bombs. At first I thought they were training aircraft, but then the bombs began to explode and people were torn to pieces. I experienced such fear that I cannot express it in words.

I barely made it home. My mother said she didn't understand what was happening, that in the morning airplanes had flown high in the sky shooting at each other. She thought it was probably training, but I said, "What do you mean 'training,' they just now bombed us!" The radio

---

[3] Constanța, Romania. The port of Constanța is the largest port on the Black Sea and fourth largest in Europe.

[4] Part of the Soviet Union's land grab following the secret protocol to the Molotov-Ribbentrop Pact it made with Germany in 1939.

announcement that the war had begun was broadcast that day.

We thought the Soviet Army was strong, that they had the best army in the world and would drive out the Germans. My father went to his work, where his boss told him to bring his family to help with removing building materials and construction equipment. A rail line had been constructed from Kishinev to Artsiz near Ukraine, and we had to take out the whole thing to transport it east. We thought we would go as far as Tiraspol and return, but when we arrived the city was under attack. A bomb fell on a large gas tank, which exploded all around and killed our leader. My father was appointed to be in charge of the train. Other than me and my parents, there was no one else on the train. My sister had married by then, and was living separately. We eventually made it to Dnepropetrovsk, where she lived. As we evacuated Moldova, bombs fell both behind and in front of us.

We continued east from there, to Krasnodar, Russia, where we were told the train would not go any further. They sent us to a collective farm, where a Cossack woman received us very warmly. She treated us with dumplings and cherries, as well as cucumbers and tomatoes, and said, "How fortunate it is you've come, Moldovans. They tell us that Jews will soon come and take our children, cut them open and drink their blood." We didn't say anything.

A week later, as the Germans approached, we decided to go deeper into the Soviet Union. That same Cossack woman said, "Where are you going, dear people? You're Moldovans, no one will harm you." But my father said, "But we're the Jews you were afraid of," and she said, "That can't be. You look like us, and we were told Jews have lots of hair and wear strange hats." My father told her that the people who dressed like that were people of faith and would never harm anyone. "Somebody simply scared you," he said.

There were a lot of people on the passenger train, so I climbed up on a third-level bunk. In the morning my entire body was covered with lice. I was disinfected at the next station, where they put all my clothes in a vat of boiling water. Lice troubled us throughout the war.

A month later, we continued east, arriving in Tashkent, Uzbekistan. We were taken to the city and then to a collective farm. A man accompanied us to a house in which no one had lived for several years, and brought us hay to sleep in. The next morning I felt something soft and warm under my leg. It turned out to be a mouse, and when we inspected the house that afternoon we found mouse holes everywhere.

We lived like this for a week, then asked the chairman of the collective farm what we could do. He said that there was a mine not far away (about 70 kilometers) where we could work and live in a dormitory. So we went to the mine. I was just twenty-one years old.

My father became a guard there, and I went to work in the open-air coal mine. My task was to open a set of doors when the coal came down after the men had blown up a certain area above me. There were horses with blinders beneath the doors, hooked to coal carts, so the coal fell through the doors into the open carts. I worked 12 hours a day doing this.

There were people at the mine who had been convicted of certain misdemeanors, such as being late for work. If you were late they took away some of your bread ration. People of various nationalities worked there, and many didn't speak Russian. I also didn't speak Russian. One woman taught me not to eat all of my bread, but to tuck a little away on my body. She said that rats can sense danger and will go to where there's bread. If I was sleeping and danger was present, the rats would wake me and I would be able to avoid it.

I worked like this for about two months, but the person who took the dynamite to the top of the mine either died or was sick, so I was put in that job. I would climb poles with a rucksack full of dynamite and give it to the miners on top. One day they didn't wait for me to climb back down, and blew up the coal just as the doors opened. I got lucky, because I was thrown through the doors into a cart along with the coal. I couldn't wait until the end of my shift, and when I arrived home I told my mother I wasn't going back to the mine, even if it meant being shot.

So I went with my pregnant sister to live with our brother in Aktyubinsk, Kazakhstan, where he was working on the railroad. He got me a job as a pre-school teacher for two- and three-year olds of varying nationalities. Like me, the children didn't speak Russian. I would feed them, give them drinks, and when they were full they would lie in my lap and I would sing Romanian songs to them.

We all ended up working on a collective farm in Kazakhstan, in terrible conditions. My father's job was to guard potato fields, and my mother would go to him during the day to fetch potatoes to boil. He was a very honest man, and would only pick up the potatoes that were on the ground. He was allowed to do this. Once, when my mother pulled up potatoes, and put them in her pocket to take home, my father told her he was a public servant, responsible for everyone, and wouldn't let her to take the potatoes. He told us to come to where he worked and we could eat there, but we were not allowed to take potatoes home.

When winter arrived and we had nothing to eat, my father went to the collective farm chairman (he was Jewish also) to ask for a little grain. The chairman said he was sure of my father's honesty, and that's why he had put him to work protecting the potato fields. The chairman said he knew my father wouldn't steal potatoes, but it was alright for our family to take some. He ordered grain for us too, and I walked 16 kilometers through mountain snow to get it to the mill. At the mill I had to use part of the grain to pay for them to grind it. We lived with constant hunger.

My sister's husband was released from the labor army and found us, then got work transporting grain at the collective farm. One day he stole a bag of grain and brought it home. My father made him return it, because we would have all been shot.

We moved again, and lived in Kyrgyzstan from 1943 to the beginning of 1944. There was a hydroelectric station being built, and they needed workers. They'd caught many Chechens and banished them to work on the station, but they were dying like flies from malaria and starvation. These fellows were worn out. My sister's job was to distribute bread tickets, giving each person that came to work a ticket for 600 grams of bread. She was required to return any extra tickets at the end of the day, and when I asked her once if we could take one ticket for ourselves and give our tickets to our parents, she refused. She said they'd put her in jail. I worked in a clinic distributing quinine for all the malaria, and took 400 or 500 grams of quinine as well.

My brother finally received notice that he could return to Moldova to work on the railroad there. He and his wife said goodbye and left, while we stayed in Kyrgyzstan: my father, mother, sister, and her little baby, who was born in 1942.

My father counted the days until the war would end. He wanted to go home very much. Our forces had already entered Hungary and Germany, and we felt the war would soon end. When construction on the hydroelectric station closed for lack of funds, we were left without food tickets.

One day a shopkeeper asked me to fix a sweater for him, because he knew I could knit. I took the sweater apart, and in two weeks knitted a new one for him. When I brought it to the shopkeeper, he gave us a piece of lamb for it. It was such a salvation. My mother cooked part of the meat and sprinkled a little grain on it, and we all ate. We put the corn we'd harvested from our garden on a couch, but ran out of corn during the winter.

One morning I tried to wake my father as he slept in his coat on a pile of hay. He didn't move, even after I touched him, and he was cold. My father had died in his sleep. When we removed his coat he was covered in lice. Someone brought a large piece of gauze for us to wrap my father in after we washed him, according to our law, and two men dug half of a grave, though they said they didn't have enough strength to continue after that. It was winter, and the ground was frozen. My sister and I finished digging the grave, and buried our father. I put a large white rock on top, but when I visited my sister 18 years later (she had stayed in Kyrgyzstan), I couldn't find the rock or the grave.

After my father died, my brother sent us money to buy grain and corn, and a cousin in Palestine found us and sent three bars of soap. It was so beautiful, shaped like eggs. We exchanged every piece of that soap for a sack of corn. And so we were saved.

One day in February 1945, as I washed up, my mother went to a neighbor for a piece of lit coal because our *pechka* had gone out.[5] We used hot coals to stoke the *pechka*, as no one had matches, but my mother tripped at the door and somehow the roof caught fire (it was made of reeds). I didn't see it, but I heard cries. When I looked out the window I saw a group of Kyrgyz people beating my mother. They believed that if a person burned their house it meant the devil was near. I ran out, naked as I was from bathing, and they saw me. I frightened them and they ran off. We moved into a dormitory at the end of the village.

---

[5] A *pechka* was an oven that doubled as a furnace. In many cases people could sleep on them to keep warm in winter as well.

That same year, my mother and I contracted typhus and were taken to a hospital, where we heard the war had ended. I was twenty-five years old by then. I was awakened by cries of joy, and looked out a window where I saw our nurse kissing the head doctor. I wondered what had happened, and the nurse ran in and said that the war had ended. It was such a blessing! When a friend told me she was leaving for Kishinev, I went to the city center to get permission to go as well. I didn't exactly say where I was going, and I received authorization.

I don't know how I made it — perhaps out of desperation. By then it was all the same to me, so I wasn't afraid of anything. I had about six kilograms of cornmeal in my bag and no money. I had nowhere to live in Kishinev, but my friend's sister was a nurse and she dragged me to a hospital, where I slept on an operating room bed. I couldn't stay permanently, and didn't know where I would live.

I was so lucky to have such good people around me: it was just amazing. There was cold and hunger in the country, and there were notes on the trees in the market with peoples names and addresses. In this way, people were able to find each other after the war.

One day, in the market, someone called my name, a woman I'd met only once in Frunze. She was the sister of a friend and told me she worked at a communist party school, teaching village students who didn't know Russian. By that time, without ever studying the language, I knew Russian. Because I also knew Romanian and Moldovan, I could translate for the students. That night I slept in a train station, and in the morning I went to the party school and was immediately hired. They gave me a dormitory room and a young there brought me a little bread. I still didn't have a ration card.

Another friend arranged for me to work as a secretary for a doctor in charge of a clinic. He tried to get me to report on what the other workers were saying about him, but I refused. He couldn't fire me because I could use a typewriter, which not many could do. After another year I became the secretary at an education and economics agency, and rented space from a co-worker.

One day I found a tomato on my desk. As it turned out, our mechanic had put it there for me. He had such bangs and was always dirty and in overalls. He carried spare parts and keys and cursed. I knew that his name was Sasha, but I didn't know that he was Jewish. Besides being our mechanic, he was also our electrician.

On the first of May I went to a demonstration, and Sasha went with me. He was clean and well dressed. He asked if he could go along with me, and I answered by saying the streets were free and he could go where he wanted. He began looking after me, bringing me various things. Once he asked me what I slept on and what I used for a blanket. All I had was my shirt. He loaned me money to buy fabric that military coats were made from. When I married him I owed him 500 rubles.

We soon had a son, and a year after that my mother asked us to come to Kyrgyzstan, where she'd stayed. We went, but only stayed one year because there was no work. We returned to Kishinev with only three rubles between us, and were given a room, a sack of potatoes, a bag of flour, and a 20-litre bottle of vegetable oil. Soon we had a daughter, and we built a house that we slowly added rooms to over a thirty-year period.

My brother left Romania for America, and lived in Detroit, Michigan. He worked in an automobile factory and I corresponded with him. He sent a request for me to visit, but the Office of Visas and Registration denied it. I went to downtown Kishinev, to the Ministry of Internal Affairs, where I saw a telephone for the Moscow Ministry of Internal Affairs and immediately called Moscow. They scheduled an appointment, so I went. I told them I had a brother I hadn't seen in 30 years, and that my husband and children would stay in Moldova. They said the Office of Visas and Registration would issue the documents, but that didn't happen until Gorbachev came to power.

In November 1991, my husband and I left for America with our daughter, her husband, and their children. My son was not allowed to come because of his health. Three months later, he was able to leave, though all that time we didn't know if they'd let him go. My husband died in 2003.

Ida Kvartovskaya

Belarus

I was born on June 16, 1939, in Mogilev, Belarus. As I was too young to remember the war, so most of these memories have been recorded by my brother, Sender. Our parents were Mordukh Aronovich Yankelevich and Gelya Issakovna, maiden name Drukman. My father was a tailor in a clothing factory, and my mother was a housewife. There were 10 children in our family: six boys and four girls. Khaim and Aron died of starvation within days of one another in 1933, when they were only a few months old. Tsilya died in 1942 during the evacuation at the age of one-and-a-half. My oldest brother, Nema (Venyamin) went to war in 1941. At first we received letters from him, but then they stopped, though we never received any news as to whether he had died. We still don't know what happened to him; there are rumors he was taken prisoner.

My grandmother (on my mother's side) had 12 children. The family was very religious and lived on the property of a synagogue. They all wound up in a ghetto where only two survived: Dodik and Basya. Basya was once pushed from a car just before someone was about to shoot her. A Russian woman took her in. After the war, Basya lived for awhile in an orphanage, and then came to live with us. She eventually married a pilot and moved to Kazakhstan. Dodik attended vocational school and returned to Mogilev after the war.

When my father found out the war had started, he decided we should hide in the woods. We stayed 10 or 15 kilometers from the city and stayed there two nights. After two days, we returned to the city, and my father returned to his job at the clothing factory. He was told at work that we needed to leave immediately, so we found a carriage for hire and went to the station, which had been bombed the night before. In the morning our neighbor Fyodor (a carriage driver) found us and asked my father to give the rest of our belongings to him. My father left with him and returned later.

We boarded a freight train. Someone had built places to sit down, and opposite the door was a gutter used as a toilet. There were men and women in one car. Soldiers in Mogilev tried to take my father from the train to send him to the war, but because he stuttered so terribly they let him go. We traded our things along the way for food at each stop. Food was available at several of the stops, which had covered areas where people could eat. When we came across trainloads of soldiers, we asked them for food, and they gave it to us. So we traveled for two weeks towards the Ural Mountains, to the city of Katav-Ivanovsk, and settled into houses there.

We wound up in a house where an old grandmother lived with her grandson. After two or three days, we went to the village of Orlovka, where we lived until December 1941. All of the children worked on a collective farm, cleaning storehouses and preparing the barns for winter. They would water, weed, and clean. There was a dining hall on the collective farm where we were fed weak soup and bread. Evacuees worked in the dining hall also.

My father's sister, Riva, lived with us as well. Her husband was forced to go to war, and her son died at Orlovka. She also had a daughter, Raya. My Aunt Riva worked in a weapons factory and watched after the children.

We moved back to Katav-Ivanovsk, where my father found work as a tailor near Zaprudovka station, and my brother Misha finished vocational school. My brother, Sender, applied to attend vocational school, and finally finished once we returned to Mogilev. My sister Sterra and I went to kindergarten.

My mother died in 1942, and my father was left alone with the children. I have absolutely no memory of my mother, as she died when I was three years old. Yet I remember my father carrying her casket on his shoulders, to where, I don't know. After my mother died, my oldest sister Yeva took care of the children and the house. I loved Yeva very much; she became a mother to me.

We heard that the war had ended on the radio. We had been living near Chelyabinsk, Russia, for four years, but following the war we returned to Belarus. By then our home was gone, and everything was destroyed. When we first arrived we had nowhere to live, so we all moved in with my mother's sister. She had a large family and so did we, so it was difficult living together.

To find a place to live, my father remarried, though I didn't like living with my stepmother because she treated us poorly. She had her children and my father had his, and in a place where the children aren't your own you can't do much. My father loved us and didn't want to hurt anyone's feelings. Eventually he left his new wife and remarried again, and again he didn't stay with his new wife long because of the children. A stepmother's a stepmother. She wanted my father's money but not his children, so I ran away from her to live with my oldest sister, Yeva.

When I was nine I became very sick and had to have an operation on my head and legs. My sister nursed me and worried about me. By the time I was nine-and-a-half, I had just started school, so it was hard for me to catch up. At sixteen, having completed only part of the seventh grade, I left school and began working in a clothes and arts factory. I worked there for 36 years as a machine embroiderer. I married, and my husband and I had one daughter and one son.

My daughter and her husband left for America with his family in 1996. My daughter immediately prepared the needed documents for my husband and me and our son's family to join them. After 14 months apart we moved to America as well, and live now in Tucson, Arizona.

Pawel Lichter

Poland

I was born on July 5, 1931, in our home in Rypin, Poland. My life there was uneventful, and everything was planned out for me, such as my future education and healthcare, and even the promise my parents had made for me to marry Renia Rosenberg, also from Rypin. Then came September 1, 1939, when the Germans marched and rolled into Poland and consequently into my hometown of Rypin – and my life changed forever.

Just before the occupation the Germans bombarded the town, and a piece of shrapnel hit just centimeters from my head as I stood in a room in our house. This would be the first of many assaults made on me by the Germans.

The Gestapo and SS came immediately after the German army, and the persecution began. My uncle, Israel Lichter, was dragged away and put in a converted enclosure along with many single, young Jewish men. They were all tortured and murdered. As for the rest of our family, we were ordered to wear yellow patches on our clothes, and the Nazis repeatedly raided and ransacked our three-story ancestral home. They took all sorts of artwork, all the silver, fur, and a very valuable stamp collection. To aggravate the situation, they ordered my father to carry all of it for them, including a safe, while they repeatedly beat, kicked, and insulted him.

The persecution continued in October 1939. My parents later told me that they and all the Jews in Rypin were obligated to "contribute" money to the Germans, who ordered the Jewish town elders to assess the contributions.

In November 1939, some of the local Germans we were friendly with before the war warned us that the Germans were about to oust all the Jews from Rypin and create a ghetto in Warsaw. They also advised us to abandon everything and head east, to Russia. They gave us *"ausweis"* (identification cards) as permission to travel. My father bought a horse and wagon, loaded us up, and we left our beautiful home and everything in it. My father also left behind the "Polina" movie house. He was a pioneer in the movie industry.

We escaped the Germans and headed toward Russia. Along the way we were stopped several times by German army patrols, each one a harrowing experience. We made it to the Belorussian border several days later, on November 11, 1939, where we were accosted by a German army patrol. They threatened and insulted us, and took whatever valuables we had left.

The German patrol then lined us up to shoot us, but at the last moment, for some reason, a German officer took a liking to my father. He called him "professor" for some reason, and told us to leave. He even pointed the way to Belarus for us. We made one last stop at a Polish farm, and the people there agreed to smuggle us into Belarus if we left the horse, wagon, and everything else. We walked through a forest for what seemed like an eternity, until our Polish guides told us we were in Russia and left. We headed for Baranovichi. I don't recall how we got there, but we did.

A Jewish family in Baranovichi took us to their home, where we lived for some time. While we were there we found out that Renia Rosenberg and her family had been sent to the Warsaw ghetto, as had the majority of Rypin's Jews. The end results of that are well known. Among those sent to the ghetto were my maternal grandfather, Chuna Bram, and his children, my aunts Rysia, Fela, and Etka.

On a spring day in 1940, at around two o'clock, Russian soldiers surrounded the house we were living in.[1] They told us we had two hours to pack, and that we were going on a trip. We were taken to the railroad station and packed into cattle cars, along with many other Jewish people, and we went on our way. After many days travel on trains, on barges down the Tavda River, and on horse-driven wagons, we arrived in

---

[1] The war between Germany and the Soviet Union began later, in June, 1941.

Kureniovo, somewhere in the Urals or Siberia, where they kept us for over a year.

In 1941 we were told we could go anywhere we wanted because we were Polish citizens and Poland was Russia's ally. My parents chose to stay as far away from the front as possible, so we went to Bukhara, Uzbekistan. We spent around five years there, suffering from hunger, sickness, and persecution. I ended up with a knife wound that became infected, and nearly died from the infection.

We were told that we could return to our home in Poland in 1946, since the war had ended in 1945. They even arranged a train comprised of cattle cars to take us for free. Our return journey was filled with further suffering, a lack of food, and other hardships. It took us over a month to return to Warsaw, and then on to Rypin.

In Rypin, we found that all the buildings and the movie house were still standing. It was impossible, though, to reclaim our properties, which had all been occupied. All of the furnishings and film equipment was missing from the movie house, which had been used by the Hitler Youth during the occupation. We decided to leave Poland as soon as we could, and with the help of several organizations and a Mexican family, an arrangement was made for us to go to Sweden, with the purpose of further transit to Mexico.

In 1947, thanks to help we received from good Swedish Jews and after obtaining visas to transit the United States, we left Sweden. We traveled on a Swedish ocean liner, the Gripsholm, destined for New York. From there we proceeded by train to Mexico City. My father, Isaak Lichter, died in 1953 from all the stress and hardship he'd endured. After he died, my mother and sister immigrated to Boston, Massachusetts.

I immigrated to the United States using a Polish visa in 1957. I could fill books with the many stories I have of hardship and suffering. Moving was a new start in life for me. I may be inaccurate in some sequences and dates, as I'm relying on my memory and what my mother, father and sister all told me. They are all deceased, so this story is being told by the only living Lichter from our Polish family.

James Lieber

Hungary

I was born on August 19, 1928, in the town of Mezőkövesd, Hungary, where I was raised as well. My name was Imre until I got to this country, where it was changed. My dad's name was Belo Lieber, and my mother's name was Leonora Lieber. Four of my brothers survived the war with me, but I lost two brothers at the front when Hungary fought the Germans and Russians. They were killed on the front in either 1941 or 1942, I can't recall now.

My birthday was actually also changed when I came to this country. I had a black spot on one of my lungs, and the counsel who gave out visas to the United States wanted to make me and my middle brother teenaged twins so he could send us without having to wait. Visas were issued according to country population, and Hungary only had eight million, unlike France and Italy with fifty or sixty million. But if you were a teenager they could give you a visa right away. My older brother Mike had to wait an extra four years to come to this country.

In early spring of 1943 they took me and my family from our small town, Mezőkövesd, to Miskolc, Hungary, a bigger city that had a ghetto. We were there approximately three weeks until a train came, and then they loaded us into boxcars with no seats. I had two grandmothers there, and they couldn't sit down. We had to stand and had nothing whatsoever, not even water, until we arrived at Auschwitz.

When we got off the train at Auschwitz, they made my father, mother, and younger brother go to the left, as I remember. Doctor Mengele made my older sister and I go to the right. I don't remember how long we stayed at Auschwitz, maybe a couple of weeks. I learned that my parents and younger brother were told they were going to take a shower, though no water came out, just gas. The gas killed them. For the next day or two you could smell the burning meat and flesh, human natures being burned. I wouldn't wish that experience on anyone. A few weeks after that, they moved me from Auschwitz to Mauthausen.[1]

Mauthausen was even worse as a concentration camp than Auschwitz, though it didn't have a gas chamber. They treated us worse than in Auschwitz, though thank G-d I only stayed there about two or three weeks. I didn't work at Mauthausen; they made me do certain things, but nobody worked there. That place was strictly used for people from Auschwitz being shifted to work camps.

I was transferred to Melk, Austria, where they had a big factory in the Alps.[2] They were digging a tunnel there, bigger and bigger, and I became a *spitzen trager*, which meant my job was to take cutting tools outside to sharpen them and return them so they could cut the bricks and wood, whatever was used in the tunnel, all day long, back and forth. They used wood in the tunnel to hold the ceilings and walls up, so we sharpened the tools outside because sparks would fly and they didn't want fires in the tunnel. I worked at Melk from 1943 to about March or April of 1945.

A German guard brought me bread every day. If they had seen him do this they would have shot him. We saw a Nazi hung once, but didn't know what he'd done. I don't know why this guard brought me bread; maybe it was because I spoke to him in Yiddish and he could understand my "German." Yiddish and German are alike. It could have been because he'd seen me at the back of a line and picked me out for whatever reason to help. I told him I was sharing with two other young fellows like myself. Sometimes he brought me a half a loaf of bread, and I told him, "The more bread you bring, the more I'm going to share it with other people." They did feed us some food to make sure we were able to complete our work for the day. All this was when I was either 15- or 16-years old.

I was capable of doing the work, although the tools were about 30 to 50 pounds, maybe more sometimes. They took any tool that had gone dull from the tunnel right away. They didn't wait, because if there were

---

[1] Mauthausen camp oversaw a series of slave labor concentration camps in German-controlled Europe. It operated under the notion of extermination through labor.

[2] Melk was a subcamp in the Mauthausen concentration camp system.

too many to sharpen they could run out of tools. They only had a certain amount of tools, maybe ten, so if one got dull they took it out to be sharpened again.

In March or April 1945, they transferred us out of Melk. We started walking towards Ebensee, about 60 or 70 kilometers away.[3] I guess Hitler was still figuring they could develop the atomic bomb so they wouldn't lose the war. They moved us because the Russians were coming from that direction.

In either May or June a unit of black Americans liberated us at Ebensee. That morning, when we woke up, we didn't see any German guards in the camp. When I saw the Americans I thought maybe all Americans were black. Four of us, all around my age, went to where the German guards had been and picked up rifles and pistols. We decided that if we saw Nazis we were going to kill them. Someone shot a man at Ebensee and I said, "You shouldn't shoot him because you don't know what he did. He might be an innocent person." I left those guys; I didn't want to stay with them.

I was looking for freight trains to get back to Hungary to see who was left in my family, because there were no regular trains at that time. It took many days to get back to Hungary, to my small town, which was on a small rail line between Budapest and Prague. So when we got to Mezőkövesd I just jumped off the train.

I reunited with my older brother Mike, my middle brother Joe, and my sister and her new husband, who she met either in the camp or afterwards. They got married in Prague, Czechoslovakia, and they came home.

There were people living in our home and in both of my grandmothers' homes. I don't remember which, but we took back one of the two homes, but only stayed for a little while there before we left. We didn't want to be there any longer because of things like this: one day I went to visit a neighbor, a doctor, and could see that the ground was all broken up where people were digging to see if others had buried their money, jewelry, or whatever. I didn't blame Hungarians for anything

---

[3]Ebensee concentration camp was established in Austria as an emergency location for the Peenemunde research center. Slave laborers dug large underground tunnels there to store armaments (such as V-2 rockets).

until I saw this. I said, "If these are the kind of people we have here, we don't need to stay here in this country anymore."

We took a train to a small town in Austria and walked across the Alps into Italy. We walked all the way to a city near the mountains, though I don't remember which city. From there we took a train to Rome, Italy. There was sort of a camp there where people like us went and applied for visas. They gave us living quarters and also fed us. Although we applied for work, after World War II there were no jobs there, even for the Italians. We stayed in Cinecittà, then applied for visas to come to America.[4]

I left Naples, Italy, in December 1946, and arrived in New York in January 1947. From there we went to Detroit, Michigan, where we had family. We stayed in a Jewish community in New York for a few days, where they put us up and fed us. When I say "we" I mean my two brothers and me. My older brother, Mike, is still alive. My middle brother, who became my "twin," has passed on. We had two uncles in Detroit, which is why my brothers and I came to this country. My sister's husband had relatives in Israel, so they went there. She passed away about six or seven years ago. She was ninety-three years old.

I was drafted in the U.S. Army during the Korean War and sent to artillery school. After I finished basic training, my company commander decided I shouldn't have to go to Korea because I'd seen enough killing in my life. Instead, they sent me to Mauthausen, Germany, the same place I'd been held by the Nazis.

After the Army I returned to Detroit, Michigan. My older brother Mike worked in a hotel as a chef with Italian and French chefs, and he became a pretty good chef. I told my uncle in Detroit: "It's so cold here in the winter. Where do they grow oranges in this country?" He said, "California, and fellows like you would go to Los Angeles." I got enough money from when I got out of the military and bought a 1947 Buick, or a Chevrolet, and I went to Los Angeles with my two brothers, Mike and Joe. I told my older brother, "You're a good chef, and we have enough money. Maybe we can open a Hungarian restaurant?"

---

[4] Cinecittà was a film studio near Rome established by the Mussolini government. From the end of WWII to 1947 it was used as a displaced persons camp for refugees.

Two whole blocks in Los Angeles had Jewish delicatessens, Italian restaurants, and Chinese restaurants, just restaurants on both blocks. Our restaurant was small, maybe about 50 seats plus the kitchen, but after two or three months people liked our food so much that they were waiting outside to get in. There was a table next to the door, so we didn't even have enough room to wait inside.

I met my wife in Los Angeles, and I wanted to have children. But I didn't want to bring any into this world after what I'd seen.

Tsiliya Lipkina

Ukraine

I was born in Gomel, Belarus, on August 18, 1923. My mother was a housewife and semi-literate. My father said he finished the fourth grade. He was a bookkeeper for the railroad. I remember that he was very well-read and had beautiful handwriting. When I was studying later at the institute in Minsk, and would write letters home, he would find my mistakes, underline them, and return the letters to me. I had a brother two years older than me and a sister three years younger. My sister lives in New York with her family; she is the person who invited us to come to America. My brother was in the war as a tank crewman, was wounded, survived, returned home, and finished law school through correspondence. He died in 1995. My mother's parents died before I was born. My father's father died when I was little, but I remember his body lying on a bed of straw on the floor. *Babushka*, my father's mother, lived with us; she died when I was in the seventh grade.

Four families lived in our communal house on Proletarskaya Street, though the entranceways were separate. I still remember it was a beautiful street near a river with many trees – a full orchard of chestnut trees. When they bloomed they were beautiful, like white candles. Old Believers lived there, and they built a church on the riverbank that has since been restored.[1] As children we would climb across a fence and pick their apples, or run to a small river and swim all day.

In 1930, by order of Stalin, all the churches in Gomel were destroyed. On our street the church was very beautiful; its high cupola gleamed like gold. We all watched them destroy such beauty.

---

[1] Russian Orthodox Old Believers (Staroveri) separated from the official Orthodox Church in 1666-1667 as a protest against church reforms.

A new, three-story school was built next to our house with two large balconies on the street and a large hall. The hall was on the first floor, with a very large ceiling and a large balcony. It was a Belorussian school, named after Karl Marx. I went to school there and graduated in June 1941. My brother also went to that school, but my sister attended the Russian school called Second Stalin School. Her school wasn't destroyed in the war, and afterwards it became a music teaching specialty school.

My mother was on the parents' committee at my school. They helped poor children by buying them clothes. Three or four years before the war, it was okay to put up a New Year's tree in school, though that was considered to be religious in nature. In our school, the upper-classmen would sit by the tree in carnival costumes, in masks, so as not to be recognized, and prizes were given to the best costumes before they took off their masks.

I wore costumes at this time of year three times from the eighth to the tenth grade. In the eighth grade I was a flower girl and wore a short skirt, blouse, and a small apron. I had a wreath of fake flowers on my head, a straw basket of fake flowers, and a mask with lace that covered my face from eyes to chin. I made the flowers myself. I received a prize, a small, light-blue box with snowflakes and waffles inside. In the tenth grade I wore a "night" costume, where I sewed stars on my mother's black dress and had a halo with a half-moon on my head.

I still remember those arduous years of famine, 1931 and 1932. It's still in my mind how my mother divided a final piece of bread into three, and I ran after my brother to exchange with him when it seemed to me that his piece was bigger. My mother would cry, not thinking of herself, only of us.

During the famine, many large cities had pawn shops where people could turn in their gold. Rich people turned in a lot of gold, which became profitable for the state because the stores paid very little. My mother had an engagement ring she turned in, though it didn't help us much. I loved my parents very much, especially my mother. From my early years I would help her. I washed the floors, though the floor was wood, not painted, and very dirty. I scrubbed it with a *derkach*, a broom made of twigs.

On June 18, 1941, we had a graduation ceremony and party, which I will always remember. Several parents brought all sorts of refreshments, to include ice cream. We danced with several officers at the party who were in Gomel to defend the railroads, transport, and bridges. The bridges and the electric station were located near the school, and their dormitory was right there as well. I had decided to apply at Gomel's Forestry Institute after school, as there were only two institutes in Gomel: teaching and forestry. My dream was to apply to study at a medical institute, but my father said they couldn't help me do that financially.

On the morning of June 22, 1941, I went to the institute to apply. I arrived, but there was nobody there because it was Sunday, so I went home. At 12 o'clock we heard Molotov's speech on the radio, in which he stated that Germany had attacked the Soviet Union. The Great Patriotic War had begun.[2] I didn't quite understand what had happened, but soon the Germans bombed Gomel, which went on every day, several times a day.

A hospital was organized at our school. The entire yard was taken up with the wounded that were lying on the ground and on stretchers. Two girls and I worked at bandaging them. The First Soviet Hospital, located near the river, was the largest hospital in Gomel. A military doctor sent me there for blood, which I carried back in two large, square bottles wrapped in a bed sheet. Night came, but there were so many wounded that they didn't all fit in the school. At night, during the bombings, the sky was lit up and horrible.

On July 6, 1941, my mother, sister and I were evacuated from Gomel in freight trains. My father stayed behind to defend the city; he wasn't in the Army, as railroad workers weren't mobilized. Later, he was sent with the Labor Army to Karaganda as a miner.

Our train stopped constantly at freight stations to let military units in trains get past us on their way to the front. The Germans constantly bombed our train, and when they did we would run from the cars. During one bombing, a woman lost her two-year-old baby in all this. My mother and I helped her search for her son, but we couldn't find him. The woman stayed behind, while our freight train continued on.

We slept in the boxcar on beds made of planks. At every station we

---

[2] "Great Patriotic War" is the term most often used for World War II in the former-Soviet Union. It is still in use today.

saw hospital trains full of the wounded. We searched for Yasha, our brother, on these trains, and my mother cried. Yasha was in the military, and served in Latvia. He was wounded in one of the first battles there, but the soldiers dragged him on an Army coat to escape being surrounded. He was mobilized in 1940, and was mature and well-educated for that time. The soldiers admired him.

Our train's final stop was at Akmolinsk, Kazakhstan. The locals told us we couldn't spend the winter there in such clothes and rubber shoes. Winter was extremely cold there, and summer was hot and dry. I was almost never home, as I immediately began searching for some kind of work.

I found a job as a bank accountant, but my salary was quite minimal. My mother cooked and my sister went to school. In the spring we planted potatoes. My mother and I had dug up the dry dirt and carried buckets of water from a stream while they grew.

I took Red Cross courses in Akmolinsk to become a nurse and wanted to go to the front. I waited to be called up, but it never happened. I donated blood every month during the war.

We returned to Belarus in January 1944. Both bridges over the Sozh River had been blown up, but the river was frozen so we walked across the ice. I saw that the school had survived, as had the First Soviet Hospital and the church near the river. All of the multi-floor buildings were blown up, and many were booby trapped. I immediately went to work in Gomel, and at the same time prepared to apply to the Medical Institute. My sister finished school while we were evacuated and wanted to apply to the Law Institute. We went to Minsk together, but since the Law Institute was no longer accepting anyone, we both attended the Medical Institute.

We began our studies in September 1944 while the war continued. Minsk was destroyed, with just the frames of buildings standing. Criminals would rob people who literally had nothing to give, just their jackets, dresses, and watches. Of all the Medical Institute buildings, only one had survived. There was a huge crater in front of one of the buildings, as big as a building, in which they'd thrown bloody bandages, splints, and human body parts. Across the street, the government building had survived.

We had no tables or textbooks, and we wrote our outlines on our knees with pens that we dipped into bottles of ink. I had a girlfriend there who now lives in Israel. She lived with her parents in Minsk and often brought me bread and butter. It was quite timely, because, as I was saying, there was nearly nothing to eat.

All the students worked to restore the city. We were given little booklets to note how many hours we worked. We dismantled the Medical Institute's buildings, brick-by-brick. We didn't have clothing, anything to eat, and received ration cards to eat at a factory kitchen. The people received cards for bread, and workers got 500 grams per day. That was the largest quota. Students were considered workers, and therefore received 500 grams as well.

During the war America sent clothing to liberated cities: dresses, blouses, and stockings. It was the first time I had seen such things. I received a beautiful blouse that was knitted red with short white sleeves, and also a beige skirt.

We knew that May 9, 1945, was Victory Day. I was in Minsk at the time, where people took to the streets all night long. Surviving officers and soldiers returned in vehicles and on foot. One vehicle stopped and snatched up four or five of us girls. We sang, danced, and had refreshments at someone's home. The soldiers, who could hardly wait for victory, had survived and were very happy to find themselves away from military action and with young girls around them. They were gentlemen, and soon moved on.

On June 29, 1949, I received my diploma for completing the full course at the medical department at the Minsk State Medical Institute. From 1949 to 1994 I worked as a doctor, and was able to work in a village hospital, a regional hospital, and in a provincial hospital. I began in the rural areas, where I saw poverty, famine, and children's diseases like the measles, diphtheria, whooping cough, and so on. I saw rural women hemorrhaging and with infection after getting abortions – which were forbidden – from women with no medical training. There were children dying because they hadn't finished treatments for diphtheria, measles-pneumonia, and scarlet fever.

My first village hospital had 45 beds for all the villages in a 50-kilometer radius. I had three people helping me: a medical assistant, nurse (the assistant's wife), and a midwife. I worked by myself all day and night in the hospital and treated everything: newborn births, broken bones, and so on.

I moved to a regional hospital in Dzerzhinsk, Minsk province, when I married in 1952. I worked there for 10 years, then moved to Gomel to work in a specialist hospital as chief of the pulmonary department. In all the years I worked in villages or regional hospitals, I never sensed anti-Semitism. But when I arrived in my own home town, Gomel, anti-Semitism was rampant, both with the people and at the institutional level. Even among the doctors I found those whose facial expressions showed me they hated us.

After my son graduated high school, he was not allowed to attend the Gomel Institute of Engineering's electro-mechanical department. He went instead to a construction institute. Once he finished there, he could only work in the factory "Tsentrolit," where the director was Jewish.

In spite of the obstacles in our home city, my son didn't want to leave, though for me it made no difference. I decided to retire at 70. My sister's children left in 1989, and my sister in 1991. They live in New York and invited us to come in 1993. My son and his wife decided to leave as well, and on June 21, 1994, we arrived in America. Sasha studied in school, then in college, yet he couldn't substantiate his Soviet credentials here. He worked for a long time at the La Paloma resort, then moved to Phoenix to work in his specialty.

My three granddaughters graduated from universities here, and my grandson is in college. I live for the sake of my grandchildren; I love them very much. We see each other once a week and I'm happy with that. When I lived in the Soviet Union, I didn't have the ability to go to Synagogue because there were none in Gomel. When my father was alive, he went to a private home to worship, had the books, and so on. I went to an American Synagogue. We don't celebrate all the holidays at my apartment complex, but we do celebrate Hanukkah and Passover. Today I baked *hamantashen* with poppy seeds; tomorrow I will take them to my granddaughter's house.[3]

---

[3] Hamantashen is a pastry in Ashkenazi Jewish cuisine recognizable for its three-cornered shape. The pastries are made with different fillings, including poppy seeds (the oldest and most traditional variety).

Yakov Makaron

Ukraine

I was born on February 2, 1923, in Zhitomir, Ukraine. My father worked as an accountant at a brewery before the war, and my mother took care of the home. In 1930, my sister Lilia was born. I remember that my father had four brothers and my mother had five sisters. I attended the Twentieth Ukrainian School, from which I graduated in 1941 before the war. Given that I was not at the draft age of nineteen at the beginning of the war, I did not serve in the army until later.

I remember that on June 22, 1941, minister of foreign affairs Molotov proclaimed over the radio the treacherous invasion of Russia by the Germans and the bombing of several cities, including Zhitomir. In reality, our city was not hit by a single bomb; the bombing occurred in an aviation town, Skomorohi, now known as Ozernoye, 12 kilometers from Zhitomir. The early days of the war brought refugees who told of horrors the Germans committed during their occupation. People were considering evacuating. One of my maternal aunt's husbands fought in World War I, and assured us that the Germans were respectable people and should not be feared. Therefore, four of my mother's sisters stayed in Zhitomir with their families, and were killed. My parents and sister also stayed and died. But I decided to flee. My parents did not fight this, and, if I remember correctly, my mother even cooked me a chicken for the road.

I fled the city on July 6, 1941, before the Germans entered the city two days later. We departed from commercial rail platforms, heading east, and the trains stopped often and became filled with refugees. I had the chance to inquire at local military enlistment offices about the possibility of joining the army. I was denied, however, because I was not yet nineteen years old and didn't have the required residence permit. I only carried my passport and a certificate proving that I was of age.

I ate at special places arranged for evacuees at large stations. I didn't want to go to central Asia, so I stopped at Chkalov, now Orenburg, and registered as an evacuee. I was sent to a far off region of the steppe called Grachevskiy, and then to a collective farm where I worked as a tally clerk and gas station attendant in a tractor crew. For the rest of that summer and into the fall I lived in a tent and later in an apartment.

I enlisted in the army at the military registration and enlistment office there. Since I wasn't clothed properly, I was given quilted pants, a jersey, and *valenki* (felt boots). I went to the regional center that provided universal education during the winter, joined the army on March 31, 1942, and attended commandeering courses in Sorochinsk, located in the Orenburg region.

After receiving approval from the credentials committee, I was sent to attend barrage balloon courses. After a week I was transferred to the radio faculty to study how to use the "Pauzo" apparatus, which controlled anti-aircraft artillery fire. Before I finished my studies, Moscow ordered the courses to be held at the Sorochinsk anti-aircraft machine-gun school, and I began studying large-caliber machine guns. I graduated from the academy in the spring of 1943.

Academy alumni were commissioned as lieutenants and sent to Moscow in boots with leg wrappings. I was selected to command large-caliber machine-gun platoon 1370, regiment 272, Yasskoy order of Kutuzov second degree anti-aircraft artillery division, the unit I was in for the duration of the war. Our division fought at numerous fronts and celebrated victory on May 11, 1945, on the border of Czechoslovakia and Austria. I was shell-shocked and awarded the Red Star, as well as a medal for military merit.[1]

After the war, our division was transferred to Rahny Lesovyie Vinnitskiy region. From there, I went to Zhitomir for a short period of time to find out what happened to my relatives. A surgeon named Gorbachesky lived near our house, who'd been there during the occupation and survived. After the war he worked in a local hospital and was awarded as a "Hero of Socialist Labor"; the hospital was also named

---

[1] The Order of the Red Star was a Soviet award given to Red Army and Soviet Navy personnel for exceptional service.

after him. But neither he, nor his wife, would tell me the fate of my parents and sister. All I could later find out was that Jewish people were told they were to be transported to a safe location, but instead were seated in cars that served as mobile gas chambers and driven to an isolated area, where six huge graves were already prepared. There's a sign now at that location that reads: "Here, Soviet citizens have been buried," and can be seen above each of the burial places without any factual mention that the people buried there are actually Jewish.

I left the army and returned to Zhitomir in July 1946, where I lived in the house that had belonged to my parents. The city's party committee, which I joined after the war, selected me to be regional administrator of the People's Commissariat for Internal Affairs.[2] Following a lengthy background check I was accepted as the operations assistant in the local police administration in January 1948. Then in 1954 a large staff reduction occurred, and I took charge of the second local police station in Zhitomir. I served in the police department for twenty seven years. During the last ten years, I worked as the deputy of the Zhitomir department of internal affairs.

I retired at 51 as a lieutenant-colonel in May 1974. Two months after retirement, I began working at a local domestic radio-electric appliances repair shop, where I stayed for twenty seven years, first as dispatcher, then as engineer of the technical department, and lastly as legal adviser. I quit in June 2001, when I was 78, because I was about to immigrate to America.

Riva Portnaya, who became my wife, worked on the railway. During the war, she evacuated with her parents to Chelyabinsk. She joined the Red Army after finishing military courses, and became a radio operator on the fourth Ukrainian front. Riva actually ran across her brother in Bulgaria during the war, whose troops happened to be there at the time. Her other brother worked as a train engineer and died during a German bombing. At the end of the war, Riva demobilized and returned to her railway work in Zhitomir. We dated for approximately a year and married in 1947, without a marriage ceremony. After we registered our marriage, we simply had lunch together with her parents.

---

[2] This is the NKVD, the public and secret police during the Stalin era. The NKVD is the precursor organization of the KGB.

We have two sons. Our older son Boris lives in Izhevsk, Russia. He has a son, who now lives in New York. Our second son, Alexander, worked in a factory in the Soviet Union, but lost his job after the country collapsed. Many plants were shut down, and he had to leave for America. Alexander now lives and works in Tucson, Arizona.

My wife became ill with Alzheimer's disease, and it became dangerous to leave her at home alone. She was not aware of her actions and needed consistent care. I had to decide whether to move to Izhevsk or to America. My brother-in-law was in Boston and suggested we come here, which we did. My wife Riva died here on August 15, 2005.

Regarding Judaism, I consider myself an internationalist: everyone was equal at school, the army was international, and I did not experience anti-Semitism in the police department. I realized later, however, that anti-Semitism and quotas for Jewish persons did exist at school and at work. When my younger son applied to Moscow Physics-Technical Institute, he received great scores on the mathematics examination yet failed the second physics entrance exam, despite the fact that he'd correctly answered all the questions. Afterwards, they asked him supplemental questions such as "Why do women like to wear red shirts?" Naturally, he did not have an answer, and the admission committee members agreed that he shouldn't pass the physics exam. A similar incident happened at a different college. I put on my military uniform to go see the college director, and specifically told him I wanted to see all of my son's entrance exams. After that, they admitted my son to the school.

I am thankful to the United Stated for the respectful and cordial attitude toward people. But, simultaneously, I experience nostalgia for my homeland. My friends are there; every corner is dear. I empathize with the people that suffer there.[3]

---

[3] Yakov Makaron passed away on November 19, 2014.

Boris Nayshtut

Ukraine

I was born in Krasnye Okny, a village in Ukraine's Odessa region, on September 15, 1935. Soon after, my father and mother moved us to Odessa. Before the war there were five people in our family: my father, Moisey Davidovich Nayshtut; my mother, Klara Viktorovna Nayshtut; my older brother, Viktor; my younger brother, Aleksander, and me. My father had 11 brothers and sisters, though only he and one brother survived the war. It was nearly the same on my mother's side: out of her 10 brothers and sisters, only two survived.

According to my father, attempts were made in approximately 1937 to stop anti-Semitism in Ukraine, and anti-Semites were even prosecuted. But before the war began, anti-Semitism had started to grow again.

The Germans bombed Odessa right after the war started, and a bomb hit my family's house at night. My younger brother Aleks and I were sleeping in a bed opposite the entranceway. The blast wave apparently tore out the door, and by some miracle the door fell onto our bed frame, blocking the ceiling above us. The house was one story, and that door held up the entire ceiling. Even today I remember when I woke up I couldn't move and began crying. I obviously lost consciousness, because when I woke up my brother and I were on the bed and our father was next to us, crying. My mother had been killed near the bed when the bomb hit the house. We were rescued and taken to a dormitory, then provided another apartment several days later.

Then another horrible event occurred: my sixteen-year-old brother, Viktor, was mobilized to defend installations at the approaches to Odessa and was killed in a bombing. We had just buried my mother. With two children (I was five and Aleks was three), my father was unable to evacuate on time.

Following my real mother's death, my father entered into a civil marriage with the woman I called "mother," as she saved my life many times. Her name was Fira Vladimirovna. Her son was killed at the same time as my older brother while defending Odessa. We were still living in Odessa when German and Romanian forces entered the city. The persecution of Jews began almost immediately.

A wave of anti-Semitism swept over Odessa. According to my parents (I write "parents" because I called Fira Vladimirovna my mother), the fascists claimed that the "Soviets" were comprised of Jews and communists. They chased the Jews away from the better neighborhoods and robbed their apartments. All across the city, the police searched homes for Jews, aided by Russians and Ukrainians. We left our apartment for Odessa's outskirts to stay with one of my father's friends, but someone told the authorities and we were taken to jail by the police with a group of Jews. At that time, jails were used as gathering points for Jews in Odessa.

Back then there were not enough workers in the villages, so in February 1942 a large group of Jews was taken to the village of Karlovka, in the Domanevsky region near Odessa. I was in this group, along with my father, mother, and little brother. My parents took up various essential jobs there, but after some time passed all of the children were taken from their parents to a farm that was far away.

At the farm, my brother and I could see that many of the children had been put into cubicles. As I remember, these were actually pigpens. Children at the farm were doomed to starve slowly, though apparently no one wanted to kill them. They simply let them quietly die. My mother made it to the farm several months later, and bribed the secret police to take my brother and me out. The guard decided she could take just one of us, and for some reason she chose me over my brother. I still remember how my mother and I crawled on the ground under the barbed wire, and how, after returning to where my parents lived, I asked if they had any *makukha* (the part left from sunflowers after the oil has been beaten from them), which I thought was the best food in the world.

My four-year-old brother Aleks didn't survive. We found out later that he starved to death on the farm. In six months our family of five was down to just two: my father and me.

My parents took part in farming and building roads. I helped to gather what remained of beets, potatoes, and so on, which we were allowed to take from the fields. Nobody brought us food. Villagers baked their own bread and traded it for clothing, and vice versa. When there was no work, my parents went to villagers and took jobs for pieces of bread, heads of cabbage, or an ear of corn. We ate whatever we could, even spoiled and rotten food.

During the occupation, my parents and I were put against the wall to be executed three times, though I will only talk about the last time, which I will always remember. It occurred at the beginning of April 1944.

My father and other men were taken to Akhmechetka to dig trenches for the retreating Germans, so my mother and I were left behind. At that time, the fascists were retreating towards Romania. A German vehicle arrived at the barracks where we lived, and once they realized we were all Jewish they rousted us out and stood against a wall. I stood next to my mother, who knew why we were standing there. At the right time, my mother told me to run to a nearby haystack to save myself. I was so frightened that I could do nothing. Everyone was forced out of the barracks as the Germans prepared for the execution. At that very moment, a second vehicle approached, and an officer told the soldiers that Soviet forces were coming and would be there any minute. The Germans quickly jumped into their vehicle, and in the meantime all the people continued to stand against the wall. The Germans only cared for their own lives. So many Jewish lives were spared in a matter of moments.

My father returned from digging trenches several days later, and we prepared to return to Odessa. On April 12, 1944, they gave the three of us documents at Karlovka stating we'd been in the ghetto since February 1, 1942. I have the documents to this day.

When we arrived in Odessa, we found out that a former policeman had taken our apartment. Realizing his situation, he moved out without saying a word. Later, he was called upon to account for occupying our apartment during the war, and after some time he was brought to justice for taking it.

Right after the war, according to my parents, anti-Semitism began to expand. By then, in Odessa, you could hear: "Jews, go away to

Tashkent," though according to military statistics Jewish people came in third within the USSR among those receiving the "Hero of the Soviet Union" award.[1]

There was a famine in 1946 in southern Ukraine, so my parents decided to move to Lvov. My mother worked in a produce store, and my father was in the printing business.

I graduated from high school in Lvov in 1954, and tried to get into the Lvov Polytechnic Institute to study mechanical engineering. But in those years, anti-Semitism was at such a high level in Lvov that you had to do extremely well when taking the entrance examinations. Even though my entrance tests were not bad, I wasn't accepted to the institute. That same year I was drafted into the Soviet Army, where I served until June 1957. That September I began working in a telegraph parts factory, where I worked for many years. I began as a locksmith, and after 16 years became a technology engineer. I enrolled again at the institute, first through correspondence courses, and then transferred to night school, which I finished in 1972.

After the USSR broke up, our lifestyle worsened significantly. Many people were out of work. I retired in 1995. In August 1993, my brother Vladimir Nayshtut (born during the war, on April 2, 1945) immigrated with his family to Tucson, Arizona. A few years later he invited my wife and me.

My wife and I arrived in Tucson on December 7, 1997. I thank G-d for this country, and that I'm able to live in this wonderful place. I've seen what freedom means to a person and to an entire country. I must confess that the first time I went to synagogue was when I came to Tucson. In Lvov, Ukraine, there were no synagogues. In Tucson, the presence of so many nearby churches made a huge impression on me. There's a Catholic church close to our house and a Lutheran church just 100 meters away. There's a synagogue located close by. As far as anti-Semitism goes, I can say that I don't feel any in my daily life here.

---

[1] The highest Soviet military award, akin to America's Medal of Honor.

Mariya Nayshtut

Ukraine

I was born in Kiev, Ukraine, on May 31, 1940. My mother was a pharmacist and my father worked as a polisher in a military factory. Before the war, my family consisted of four people: my father, Motel Yankelevich Perel; my mother, Cherna Yankelevna Perel; my older brother, Yankel Motelevich Perel; and me. My mother had five sisters and six brothers. All of her brothers and her older sister were killed during the war. My father had one brother and one sister who remained in Kiev. I was one year old when the war began, so what I'm writing is what I recall from my parents.

The Germans acted out against Jews immediately after occupying Kiev. Jews were taken to Babi Yar in large groups, where they were executed.[1] My uncle's family was among them. At Babi Yar, where the fascists stood people near ditches to shoot them, my uncle's son, Iosef, stood next to his father, waiting. But when the shots began, he and another boy simply fell into the ditch on top of the dead bodies. After the executions, the ditch was filled in, but by some miracle the boys managed to dig their way out and run into the woods, where partisans found them. That's how my cousin survived.

At one point a message arrived regarding my mother's brother, Isaak, who was a tank crewman. He blew up his own tank rather than surrender it to the Germans. I must repeat: all six of my mother's brothers were killed in the war.

---

[1] Babi Yar is a ravine in Kiev, and the site of massacres carried out by the Germans against Ukrainian Jews. The most notorious occurred 29-30 September, 1941, when nearly 34,000 Jews were killed in a single operation.

Immediately after the war began, the factory where my father worked was to be evacuated to Kuybyshev by order of the government. Before that, as my father worked one night, several people knocked on our door and asked my mother "Do Jews live here?" My mother said yes, and asked what they wanted. A man said they'd return the following day to kill us. This was the state of anti-Semitism in Ukraine. That night, my father said we should gather our things as quickly as possible, as there was a train at the station for factory personnel headed to Kuybyshev.

As my parents explained it, my mother carried me in her arms, my five-year-old brother carried two packages, and my father balanced a child's washtub on his head with luggage in both hands. We left the city at night, loaded onto a train, and departed.

The factories were transferred to outlying villages near Kuybyshev. My father worked in the large military factory, two or three shifts at a time without a break. My mother worked in a factory as well. It was very cold, and there was no food. My mother had a daughter in 1943. We had nothing to eat, and the children went hungry.

My father sometimes brought vodka home from the factory, which my mother traded for bread and soup. One time she dug up several potatoes from a field, but a guard saw her and told her to leave or they'd turn her over to a military tribunal, meaning she'd be shot on the spot.

We returned to Kiev in 1946, but our apartment was occupied by some sort of higher up and we couldn't get it back. My parents decided to go to Lvov, Ukraine, since three of my mother's sisters lived there. Our family of five received a room in Lvov that was 9.5 square meters (102 square feet). We lived in this room for 14 years.

I graduated school in Lvov in 1958 and went to work in a military factory, where I worked as an operator in the computer center for 37 years. I retired when I was 55.

There has always been anti-Semitism in Western Ukraine, with its center in Lvov, and for many years it will be a breeding ground for anti-Semitism. I always had to remember that I was Jewish in the factory, and had to work better than my colleagues. This meant never being late, never leaving work early, maintaining quality work, and behaving.

My husband and I moved to America in December 1997. We are very lucky to live in this country.

Adelya Plotnikova

Ukraine

I am Adelya Isaakovna Plotnikova, maiden name Zhvanetskaya, born June 12, 1935 in Odessa, Ukraine. My father, Isaac Zhvanetsky, was a locksmith.

My mother, Ida Zhvanetskaya (maiden name Maidenberg) was a sort of petty bourgeois who'd owned a dye shop and a building with 30 apartments in Moldavanka (an area of Odessa where poor and middle class people lived) prior to Soviet rule. Once the Soviets took over, her shop and the apartment building were nationalized, and she lived in a one-room, 30-square meter apartment (340-square feet). This was the same home we lived in just before the war began in 1941.

At the end of 1917 my father's parents and his younger brother, Yakov, secretly crossed the border and immigrated to America, leaving my father behind with his grandmother. In 1918, after his grandmother died, my father made several attempts to cross the border, but was returned. He ran off to the front and became a "regimental son," though he fell ill with typhus and was sent to the rear, where he was sent to an orphanage. In 1922, when he turned eighteen, my father was selected to go to technical school to specialize in metal repair and manufacturing for keys and locks.

There were five people in my family prior to the war: my father, mother, grandmother, my older sister (born in 1930), and me. On my father's side, I had an uncle with whom my father did not have a relationship, while on my mother's side I had my Aunt Asya Gorina (my mother's sister), her husband Mikhail Gorin, their son (my cousin) Gedeon Gorin, and my mother's brother, Mikhail Aronovich Maidenberg. On June 12, 1941, I turned six years old. The war began 10 days later.

We first heard reports of the war from the Soviet Information Bureau. In the first days of the war my father, brother, and my aunt's husband were all mobilized and sent to the front. My father went to defend Sevastopol. My mother, like other able-bodied residents in Odessa, was sent to dig anti-tank trenches at the outskirts of the city. She was rarely home, so my sister and I stayed with our grandmother. During the bombings (which occurred several times a day), we hid in an entranceway with a concrete ceiling or in the catacombs beneath our house. We experienced indescribable fear from the wail of sirens and the sounds of approaching enemy aircraft.

In early August 1941, my father's regiment moved from Sevastopol to defend Odessa, where he was wounded on August 19. He was sent to an evacuation hospital, since they knew Odessa had surrendered to the enemy. When the Germans were close to Odessa – 40 kilometers away in the village of Dalnik – the order came to evacuate the hospital by ship to Novorossiysk. My mother, who worked in a hospital, hurriedly gathered the children and the most necessary items. The family – my wounded father, Aunt Asya, and her son Gedeon – and others from the hospital sailed on the ship under the cover of night in the early days of September 1941.

At dawn we were attacked by German fighter aircraft. Several miles ahead of us, the steamship Lenin was sunk right before our eyes, though we were unable to help those who were drowning.[1] Thanks to the guns mounted on our ship, we avoided the Lenin's fate, but during one bombing I received shrapnel wounds to my left foot.

Once we arrived in Novorossiysk, my father was sent to Voroshilovsk, where a commission found him unfit for military action and certified him as being disabled. He was sent for treatment to Tashkent, Uzbekistan, where he remained until the end of 1943.

We reached Tashkent via Stavropol on freight trains. To avoid attacks the trains often switched tracks, and during one such maneuver we lost my mother and Aunt Asya, who'd run off to the station for hot water. Thanks to the train maneuvering, my mother and aunt hopped on its step as it moved and miraculously survived. It was –25 degrees Celsius

---

[1] According to one historian, the Lenin was likely sunk by a Romanian submarine. As many as 4,600 passengers died.

(-13 Fahrenheit), and they had to warm their hands with their own breath because their hands were stuck to the metal. They prayed to G-d they didn't fall.

Along the way, my cousin Gedeon and I became ill with typhoid fever, and Gedeon died. He was buried somewhere on the Orenburg steppe, wrapped in a towel in a hastily dug pit.

Toward the end of December 1941, after four months, we arrived in Tashkent, where we met my father in the hospital. My mother worked again as a nursing aid in a hospital. My sister and I went to school, though in our spare time we cared for the wounded. My father was discharged from the hospital in 1943, but still couldn't physically work. He completed a quick course in tax finance and went to work as an agent at the Regional Finance Department.

The long-awaited news of victory came in May 1945, and at the beginning of 1946 we returned to Odessa, where our ransacked apartment was occupied by other tenants, though they returned it to us. In Tashkent we had heard about the horrors that had befallen Ukrainian Jews at the hands of the Germans and the Ukrainians, though we couldn't imagine how. In Tashkent a friend of my father's, an Uzbeki national, had proposed that my father change his nationality and stay. He predicted that nothing good awaited the Jews in their liberated nation after the city's occupation. But my father refused, saying his nation would not betray him.

My younger sister, Ira Zhvanetskaya, was born in Tashkent in 1944. In Ilichevsky region my father worked in a finance department and at the same time studied through the credit and financial correspondence technical college. My older sister and I continued going to school, while my mother, our grandmother, and my little sister stayed home. We lived very poorly; my mother did all the housework and sewed our clothes for everyone from oldest to youngest.

My sister graduated from the Credit-Economic Institute and was sent to work in Pyshma, in Sverdlovsk region. She had a nervous breakdown several months later from all the persecution she received for being Jewish. After taking her away from there, my father put her in a neurological clinic for treatment.

I studied refrigeration at a technical college in Odessa starting in

1949. I passed the entrance exams, and because there was a shortage of students I was enrolled. Before that I'd taken the entrance exams for the Machine Tool Technical College, but I was intentionally disqualified in the last test. From then on, I was aware of what it meant to be Jewish in the Soviet Union.

I graduated from technical college in 1954 with honors and was sent to the Odessa Technological Institute for Refrigeration with the right to enter without having to take the entrance examination. Of the five students who graduated with honors, two were Jewish: myself and Alexander Sagalevich. When Alexander was refused entry, I wrote a complaint to the Ministry of Education, but to no avail.

After working nearly eight years at the Lvov mechanical-repair factory, I returned to Odessa to work as foreman in a plant that constructed and repaired equipment for the food industry. I worked 36 years there, right up until I departed for America. I was often awarded for good work, and received the "Highest-Level Master" medal and a free trip to tour Bulgaria in 1980. But the award was rejected by the committee chairman of the regional food union industry because I was Jewish.

I explained the whole thing to the committee chairman of the regional trade union, telling him just what I thought about such anti-Semites like he and his ilk. I also wrote a letter of complaint to the Ministry of Food, in which I explained that my father was a disabled veteran who hadn't fought for his country just so his children could suffer in their homeland for being an objectionable nationality in that country.[2]

My relatives were, of course, terrified by my actions, and expected some sort of repressive measures, but they didn't happen. I received a letter from the ministry, an invitation to the regional committee of trade unions, and a free trip to the GDR.[3] But I didn't go, as my parents were seriously ill.

After my parents died my older sister went to America to reunite with her son, and after that I became fixed with the idea that I would say goodbye to my country. The final push was an incident with a neighbor who threw a stray puppy from a fifth-floor apartment as I watched.

---

[2] The Russian Empire, and the Soviet Union, considered Judaism a nationality.
[3] GDR was the German Democratic Republic, or East Germany

When I said that was how the fascists acted, he called me a dirty Jew and said I should go to Israel. I slapped him. I never gave in to anti-Semites, and I never let those who humiliated my dignity go unnoticed.

My dream came true in 1998 when I received permission from America to enter the U.S. as a refugee. I am eternally grateful to America for its warm welcome, for the fact that I am surrounded with care in my old age, for the fact that my grandchildren can go to university here, and because they won't experience humiliation like I did. What happened to me — and those like me — can never be forgiven or forgotten.

Mikhail Rabinovich

Ukraine

I was born in 1930 in Chernigov, Ukraine, into the family of a laborer. My mother was a housewife, so it fell on her to take care of the family and her sick mother, who could hardly get around. There were three boys in the family: I was the youngest; the oldest was ten years older than me; and our middle brother died in an absurd way in 1934, when the doctor wasn't attentive enough after my brother stepped on something. He died of blood poisoning two days later. Right up to the war my parents had still not gotten over the terrible shock.

I was eleven years old in 1941, and in the third grade. On June 22, 1941, our class was on a field trip to see a movie, and while we were watching it we heard that the war had started. No one thought or knew what might happen next. Our relatives came to our home, and our friends were discussing what to do, where to go and where to stay, and what would happen to our sick grandmother. My father remembered that during the First World War the Germans didn't bother the Jews. But after a few weeks, refugees began arriving from other areas, and among them were many orthodox Jews telling us how the Germans were persecuting the Jews. We decided to leave.

Organizations and factories were leaving. My father worked at an Artel, where there were stables with horses and carts.[1] We had our own horse and wagon, and the Soviets had created an Artel where Jews stabled their horses. My father went to work and came home with the horse and wagon, telling us that the authorities had all fled and people had taken the horses. We loaded some of our belongings and put our grandmother on the wagon, and in the course of three weeks reached

---

[1] An Artel is a general Soviet term for various cooperatives.

123

Voronezh. That was August 1941. As we left, we could see that Chernigov was on fire.

We went to Otrozhka station near Voronezh, where they'd formed trains for evacuating refugees. The trains had boxcars used to transport cattle but had been converted to carry people. We loaded up, and after a month and a half were at the edge of Southern Kazakhstan. Our train was coupled and uncoupled repeatedly, maneuvering in order to avoid being bombed.

We arrived at Mirka station, 200 kilometers from Dzhambul.[2] The village there, Kuzminki, was a post-revolutionary settlement of former-Russian and Ukrainian *Kulaks*.[3] We were put in a small "saman," a duplex-type cottage. What is a "saman"? It's a home made from bricks that are created by mixing straw with clay solution, both roof and floor covered with the clay. The floor had to be redone each week, so we prepared the clay solution ourselves and smeared it on.

The climate was hot: the summer heat was somewhere around 40 degrees Celsius (104 Fahrenheit), and the winter was cool but without snow. We had to survive somehow, so my father worked as a cattleman on a ranch that belonged to a sugar factory. They fattened the cattle as a supply for canned meats sent to the front. We kept warm with straw, and deadwood known as "Kurai" (connected with bundles of straw and other deadwood).

I would go to school and after lunch help my parents. Shortly after we arrived my grandmother died, and my mother suffered from heart failure, so our needs fell to my father and me. My older brother was drafted into the army in 1940 and served in the Far East, but was transferred to the front at Stalingrad. He was seriously wounded in 1942, but recovered. In 1944 he transferred to the reserves, found out where we were through the Red Cross, and traveled there.

We were given land and grew corn, which we were allowed to water only at night. We gathered and shucked it, then ground the corn into flour with two stones. We also received bread with our food ration cards.

---

[2] Dzhambul, now called Taraz, is a city in southern Kazakhstan.
[3] *Kulak* is a Tsarist Russian term for affluent farmers, expanded during Soviet rule to include nearly any peasant landowner. The Soviet Politburo approved the extermination of *Kulaks* as a class in early 1930.

By the end of 1944 we felt the war was coming to a close and decided to return to Chernigov, where we had a home, and applied for permission to return. When we returned, at the end of 1945, we found that our house had been completely plundered. We were told that Germans had been billeted there. I went to work as an apprentice plumber in a factory and studied at night school up to the ninth grade. I took my tenth grade examinations without attending school.

Shortly after the war we buried my mother. She'd had two strokes. My father was alone. My brother married and went to America with his wife and their two daughters. I attended the Romny Military Automobile School to become an engineer-mechanic, graduating with honors. I got married before I graduated.

Based on my choice, I was based in Kiev and all across Ukraine. I also worked on the Kamchatka peninsula and Sakhalin Island.[4] On Kamchatka (13 kilometers from the city center of Petropavlovsk-Kamchatsky), I was chief engineer of an automotive repair battalion, and was then transferred to Sakhalin Island, where I received the rank of major. I served six years there, then transferred again to Kamchatka. Our son Aleksander completed the tenth grade there.

I finished my service at the rank of major, and received a three-room apartment in Kiev. I worked as a civilian in a factory supply department, where I managed the component supply and spare parts after the design department made their requests. I supervised a group dealing with supply requests related to quotas.

It was at this time that my family considered the issue of leaving Ukraine. In 1989, our son Pavel, who was a computer programmer, received his immigration approval from Israel. They waited in Italy for approval to go to America, then went to New York once that came in.[5] He then invited us to join his family. We knew we were going to Tucson while we were still in Ukraine. Pavel would visit us in Tucson until he moved here himself. Of course, it was difficult to register the customs documents, but we got through it and found our new homeland in 1991.

---

[4] Kamchatka and Sakhalin island are in the Russian Far East.
[5] In the 1980s and early 1990s, Soviet Jews were usually unable to immigrate directly to the United States. Instead, they applied for Israel, then further applied for America once physically out of the Soviet Union.

We were well met in America. Separate apartments at "La Mirada" were prepared for my wife and me and for our son Aleksander's family. We soon went to work selling flowers and bought a car. Eventually we opened an automotive business and opened a store, "European Market." I worked at the store for awhile, though now our son Aleksander and his wife manage the store.

Here's another thing I want to say: thank you America, for providing for us in our old age.

Klara Raykh

Ukraine

I was born on November 14, 1926, in the city of Pervomaysk, Ukraine. I was the only child of Bentzion and Etya Timen. I was fifteen years old when the Nazis attacked the Soviet Union on June 22, 1941. My father was immediately drafted into the Soviet Army, while I remained with my mother.

On June 27, 1941, the Germans began bombing Pervomaysk. My mother and I were very frightened and defenseless, so we decided to leave as soon as possible. We could not take anything with us except our documents and the coats on our backs. My mother and I walked for many long hours, looking for somewhere to hide in the countryside. It was early July 1941. We hid in village cellars for several days. The Nazis came to the area desperately searching for Jews to eliminate. They wanted to find as many of us as possible. By some miracle, my mother and I escaped, but my mother's sister, her husband, and their two little daughters were killed by the fascists.

We were stuck in that region for two months, as it was occupied by the Nazis and we couldn't get out. We walked from one village to another in the dark of night (it was too dangerous to travel during the day) begging local people for small amounts of food and shelter in which we could hide. Finally, sometime in September 1941, partisans found us. They gave us something to eat and put us with other refugees on a horse-drawn wagon that was secretly headed for Kharkov.

We had to stay in Kharkov for a few weeks because all the trains to the Asian and Siberian regions of the country were overcrowded. Soon the Germans started bombing Kharkov as well. We finally managed to get on a train from Ukraine to Uzbekistan in early October 1941. By then Ukraine was almost completely under Nazi control.

We reached Uzbekistan in November 1941, and stayed a few weeks in Tashkent. We then went to Yangiyul, Uzbekistan. It wasn't until December or early January 1942, that we managed to reach Novosibirsk, in Siberia, where we stayed with relatives until 1943. I was sixteen years old and worked in a factory there, taking some classes in evening high school. We didn't hear from my father for two years, and didn't know that he'd been severely wounded and was in a hospital. And he didn't know whether or not we were alive or had escaped the Nazi invasion. It was only at the end of 1943 that he found us, and in 1944 we reunited with him and moved to Kuybyshev, where my father worked as editor of an Army newspaper.

We never managed to return to our home in Pervomaysk. It had been burned to the ground, and all of our belongings were stolen or lost. Most of our relatives and friends there were killed by the Nazis. So we went to Odessa after it was liberated from the Germans and Romanians. That was where we celebrated the war's end in May 1945.[1]

---

[1] Klara Raykh passed away on November 7, 2013.

Sara Rozenfeld

Ukraine

I am Sara Rozenfeld, born in 1923 in the city of Pervomaysk, Ukraine, Odessa region (now Nikolaevsk region). Our family was small: my father, mother, and me. My father was a bookkeeper and my mother was a housewife. I graduated from the tenth grade in 1941 and was ready to enter a medical institute. That was on June 19, 1941. The morning after our graduation party, we heard the news of Germany's sudden attack on the Soviet Union. The war began on June 22, 1941.

This caused fear, anxiety, and feelings of helplessness. German aircraft were soon bombing the city, and German artillery began firing on us. Their goal was to destroy the bridge over the Bug River, and because we lived in that area we were subjected to constant danger. One of the first bombs fell in our courtyard. The building shook, and there was a huge crater, but our home was still standing and so were we. G-d himself had obviously saved us.

There was a panic in the city. German propaganda played on personal radios, appealing to the Ukrainian locals not to leave their homes because Hitler was only after the Jews and communists. It became dreadful to stay at home, and we realized that we had to leave Ukraine.

Because of his age, my father didn't work and wasn't called up to the Army. He went to the train station and found out that the last trains were leaving, that after that all train movement would stop. We prepared quickly, using old clothes to make bags and throwing warm clothes into them. We added rope to carry the bags on our backs. It constantly rained that summer of 1941, it was cold and wet. We took the vinyl tablecloth from the kitchen, but left everything else at home when we went to the train station.

Prior to leaving, my mother baked *lepyoshkas* out of the flour and water we had left.[1] There was a train at the station with four open-air cars and three iron cars for hauling coal and other loose loads, which were also open-air. Our aunt's family of three joined us. To our good fortune, our boxcar was connected to a train headed east, to a Machine Building Plant in Orenburg. The trip was very difficult, and we were bombed several times along the way. The train would stop and they'd turn out all the lights and the train's furnace. They'd order us off the train to run into a field, where we'd lie on the ground until the raid was over. It took us two weeks to get to Orenburg.

We were sent from Orenburg to Kubandyk, on the Sakmara River, where there was a logging village. A year later the Kiev Mechanical Factory transferred there. It had been converted to a military factory that made antitank grenades and hand grenades for the front. I soon started working there, first as a laborer and then as a drafting technician. The work was not easy. We worked three shifts in difficult conditions without counting our hours, until we used up all the available materials. Most of us were young.

After the war ended in 1945, I went to study at the Orenburg Medical Institute. After three years there, I transferred to Odessa Medical Institute, and our family returned to Pervomaysk. I graduated in 1950 and married Abram Wiseman, who graduated from Odessa Pedagogical Institute. We were sent to work in a village located in the Izmailsky region, where we stayed for eight years.

The creation of the state of Israel gave us great joy and pride, and we decided to go there once the chance arose. In 1998 we departed for Israel. Our daughter and her family left for America at that time, and in 2010 our family finally reunited in Tucson, Arizona.

---

[1] *Lepyoshka* is a type of round bread.

David Rubinstein

Ukraine

I was born in the village of Zalivayshchino in Ukraine's Vinnitsa region. My father was a village store manager and was sent there to organize Soviet trade in the area. My parents were from Novokonstantinov, in Ukraine's Proskurovsky region.

In 1940 we moved to Kiev, since that's where all of my relatives lived: my grandfather on my mother's side and my mother's sisters. We were in Kiev when the war began, in June 1941. I was eight years old at the time.

On August 20, 1941, with battles occurring at the outskirts of Kiev, our family – my mother, sister, brother and me – evacuated Kiev on one of the last trains leaving the city. My father had been called into the army. We were put on open-air, half-rail cars normally used for transporting coal. Some members of my family were not able to evacuate. The Germans hung one of my aunts and threw my grandparents down a well, where they died.

Our train was bombed many times during the evacuation. The train was hit near the city of Konotop, and part of a shell shattered my mother's leg. At night, as the train burned, peasants from a nearby local village helped us, and took us to their village. On August 30, 1941, German soldiers parachuted into the area, capturing the village. Still, the peasants hid us. These were difficult days for my family. We lived with a real fear that they would find us and kill us.

In October 1941, a Soviet Army unit came to the village trying to evade German capture. My mother asked their commander to take us with them. He looked after us and placed us on wagons carrying wounded soldiers. Thanks to the Soviet soldiers, we made it to the train station at Bakhmach.

From there we went to Ostrogorsk, in the Voronezh region, where one of my grandfathers was located. After we arrived, everyone was sent on to Ural. My uncle worked in a military plant that was transferred to Izhevsk. We remained in Ostrogorsk, because we had no clothes and nothing with us.

The Germans approached Voronezh in 1942, so we decided to evacuate to central Asia, to Uzbekistan. We rode in boxcars, and I became sick with Scarlet Fever. I was sick for a long time from the conditions in the boxcars.

We made it to Tashkent, Uzbekistan, and were told to go to Syrdarya, an area infected with malaria. The disease tortured us. We drank ditch water and fell sick with dysentery, and suffered with hunger for two years. For the first year and a half, sick and exhausted, I didn't go to school. My health remained poor even when I finally did. Our mother was bedridden from wounds that hadn't properly healed because of a lack of available medical care. She couldn't work. My sister made rope for the war and went to school, and my brother worked and attended technical school. I was too small to work.

After the war my father was demobilized. He found out where we'd gone and came there for us. He found work as an overseer at the Central Growing Station in Tashkent, where they grew cotton. He took me with him when he left for Tashkent, while my mother and sister remained in Syrdarya because my sister was finishing high school.

In Tashkent, my father would go to work while I waited all day for him to return. I went to school there, where they gave us 125 grams of bread. In 1945, while still at the cotton station, it was announced that the war had ended. We chose to stay in central Asia, where I graduated from high school.

I attended the Tashkent Polytechnical Institute, where I studied electrical power systems. I graduated in 1957, and worked with diesel locomotives in Novosibirsk after that. My wife and I have three daughters. Our family arrived in the in the United States in 1993.

Eva Siebert

Hungary

I was born on April 17, 1918, in Budapest, Hungary.[1] My father was Elgin Rod, a lawyer, and my mother's name was Gabriella. I was raised by my grandparents, very intelligent people who were doctors. I went to an orthodox school for eight years in Budapest, then to a boarding school in Vienna, Austria. When I was twenty I received my teaching certificate, then taught in a Montessori school for children.

I married on February 1, 1939, and on February 23 the grandmother who raised me from the age of four died. After my husband and I married we lived on his land, 400 hectares[2] that we farmed. We had 16 Lipizzaner horses, one male and 15 female, which we bred. We would sell a horse once it turned four, and my husband taught people how to ride them properly. These horses could lose their self-confidence if someone struck them. We lived on the farm until June 1, 1944, when I had to go into hiding.

Prior to that, when the Jewish rule came out, people who knew me began to walk on the other side of the street so they wouldn't have to say hello. This was what life became. My grandparents were such good people, and helped everybody, and they couldn't believe what was happening. My grandfather was an important person, but after Passover that year he was taken away. He arrived at Auschwitz on June 22, 1944, and he left us a letter that said, "I'm going to Germany, where they're not going to love me or feed me. I will die there." He was eighty-three years old, and they killed him right away.

---

[1] Ms. Siebert is the mother of Theresa Dulgov, whose story is also featured in this collection.
[2] Equates to 988 acres.

133

My father was very headstrong. When Czechoslovakia took Košice, he was only 20 miles away, but he refused to speak Slovak.[3] He spoke many languages, and this is why he refused. One November night they took him to Košice and punished him for this reason. There was a Hungarian group of Slovak gangsters, led by Jarosh Andras, who became a minister during the Nazi times. Jarosh Andras gave my father a paper stating that he was a well-respected Jew, not an ordinary Jew (because my father was the secretary of the Hungarian group). I kept the paper with me at all times, because as long as no one took it I'd be alright. My father died anyways.

I went into hiding in 1944. My husband couldn't hide, because he had to wear the Jewish star. I didn't have to wear the star because I had that paper from my father. I wanted to go to a town where the people didn't know me, then go to Budapest where my mother was living with my uncle and other family. When I got on the train, the Hungarian gendarmes were there looking for Jews. The Hungarian gendarmes were horrible people, worse than the police. I was nine months pregnant and turned white with fear because of them. There were also two German SS men on the train, and I spoke perfect German, so I fell down on the bench, on purpose, and the SS men started talking to me. I told them I was expecting a baby and they put their jackets around me, and tried to nurse me. The Hungarian gendarmes gave them the Nazi salute and left.

When we arrived in Budapest there were gendarmes everywhere, but I had these two German Nazis with me, carrying my bag. I looked Jewish, but who would dare ask the SS about it? I said I had to go to the hospital, which they knew. Only Germans could use the taxis so they got one for me. I got in the taxi, but went to see my mother instead.

My mother took me to the university hospital instead of the Jewish hospital. The doctor there was a Nazi, but the doctors swore not to give anyone up as long as they were ill. I had to have a Caesarean section, because the birth went very badly. I was in the hospital for three weeks and was between life and death.

By that time the Jewish star was already on all the houses. The

---

[3] The border areas between Czechoslovakia, Hungary, Poland, and Ukraine shifted numerous times during this period, which often resulted in attempts to force the halt of native languages. Košice is now part of Slovakia.

troubles began when I moved to my mother's house. I asked my governess, a Lutheran, what I should do with my child, and she told me not to worry, that she knew a place where we could stay. She had a guest house, and though they knew I was Jewish they hid me there. Someone was living in the room next to mine, Mr. Rózsavölgy, who had the largest office complex in Budapest. He was living there with his wife and two children. He worked for the Swedish Red Cross and took me to see Wallenberg, who gave me money each week to live on while I hid.[4] After Hungarian President Mikos Horthy stepped down, on October 15, 1944, my father was taken away. Jarosh Andras was now a nobody, and I still had no idea where my husband was, or even if he was alive.

On July 10, 1944, they caught my mother at my aunt's house, where she was staying. My grandmother was in the ghetto, and they beat her so badly that she told them where her daughter was, so they caught my mother. They took my mother to Auschwitz on August 4, 1944, which was Tisha B'Av.[5] She was forty-eight years old, but her hair was gray so she was killed. Other women that same age – her girlfriend and my school teacher – survived. It was because her hair was gray. They didn't even put her into a work camp, she was killed right away.

The Swedish Red Cross had given me a place to hide with the nuns. There were another 10 or 12 people with babies hiding there, and maybe 150 babies without parents. They told me they'd keep me safe and let me live in the house that they lived in. I didn't have any winter clothing, and had to put newspaper pages on the bottoms of my shoes because the soles were gone.

On November 27, 1944, they caught me. They took the paper that my father had given me, along with everything I had, and prepared to take me to G-d knows where. An elderly woman in the group I was in fell down, and the Nazis began to beat her. When I saw this I thought, "I don't care, I'm not dying. I will survive Hitler." I was twenty-six years old with a six-month-old baby. There was a Hungarian policeman there, so I

---

[4] Raoul Wallenberg was a Swedish diplomat who saved thousands of Jews in Nazi-occupied Hungary during World War II. He was detained by the Soviets after the war and is reported to have died in Lyubyanka prison in Moscow.
[5] Tisha B'Av is a day of fasting. It commemorates the destruction of the First and Second Temples in Jerusalem, and the exile of the Jews from the Land of Israel.

stood next to him. I put down baby food that I'd gotten, then slowly and calmly walked away. I had no money, but I had a daily use transportation card that I used to get the baby food. I got to the subway station and left.

When I got home the nuns told me I could no longer stay with them. The Germans, they said, were coming for everyone. So I hid on the roof, where it was windy and snowy, and where the rain came down. I didn't even have a coat. I hid there until February 3, 1945.

Each day I had to go for two pails of water, and I did this with a girlfriend who had an eight-year-old boy and a ten-year-old girl. My girlfriend's name was Agnes. On January 13, we went to the Danube River for water, where Agnes said she'd step down to the river and hand the pails of water up to me. We had on white sheets to hide, because there was snow, but we saw some kind of movement in the area, which turned out to be a soldier. He didn't know who we were, and he shot at us. Agnes was killed with a bullet.

I wasn't always afraid of going out. I had another friend there, a woman with two little girls whose father was a Nazi SS soldier. Every night I had to go to him to get food for his children, and he would give me extra food for my daughter. I was never frightened; if you became frightened you could get killed. When something started going wrong I'd stop and go back. I'm a fatalist.

The convent was falling to pieces, its windows and doors gone. They freed the people from the ghetto on January 18, 1945, and on February 12 the Russians took Budapest. That first night, three young Russians came in, tossed my baby to the side, and all three of them raped me. I thought I might not live another day after that, I was just crazy. I couldn't live in the convent another day, so I went to my uncle and his Christian wife, but they told me I couldn't stay with them.

I had very little food, and what food I could get I gave to my baby. I would toast bits of food and put it in a handkerchief, then give it to my baby, who would suck on the handkerchief. So I was very hungry. I went to stores looking for food, and even stole a jar of mustard just so I could lick it when I was hungry. That February I went to a home in Budapest and told them I was Jewish and in hiding. I said I needed a home for my child. They found space for me.

My husband returned to our home and sent someone to Budapest to look for me. A friend of my sister-in-law's was in that home with me, and they found us there. The first day the bridge was available was March 24, 1945, and I crossed it that day. I went to Chepel, a twenty-two-kilometer trip, with a baby around my neck and no food.[6] My baby is 65-years old now. She was born June 24, 1944. It took three days to get home, because the train was an old-fashioned locomotive, and when it traveled uphill everyone had to get out and push.

My husband cried and people ran up to us when we arrived home. It was the first time he'd seen his child, who was by then eight months old. I didn't have shoes or clothes, and the baby only had two diapers. I waited a whole year for my mother to come home, because I thought she was young enough to survive. I sat Shiva for the whole family after that.[7]

The people in our town were very friendly, they loved my husband. We had always lived there. The intelligent people were the ones who didn't like us, because they'd been Nazis. The peasants were never Nazis. My husband kept bees, so we had honey. We had no sugar or salt, but we did have potatoes and corn. So we did have some food. My second daughter was born in 1946.

The Russians eventually put my husband in jail because he owned land, calling him a "stinking Jewish *kulak*."[8] He was released in the 1950s, but he'd been given injections in prison. He was poisoned there. He died in a Hungarian hospital in 1956, where he spent 11 months.

On December 8, 1956, I left Budapest with my daughters, a nine-year old and an eleven-year old, for Győr, Hungary. We walked to Austria from there along with hundreds of other refugees, and though the Russians caught people in front of us and behind us, they never caught us. After a month in Eisenstadt, Austria, we found out we were too late to go to America, but heard that the Portuguese might be able to help, so we went to Portugal. We were there nine months before we returned to Austria.

---

[6] An area of Budapest.

[7] Shiva is a week-long period of mourning in Judaism.

[8] *Kulak* is a Tsarist Russian term for affluent farmers, expanded during Soviet rule to include nearly any peasant landowner. The Soviet government approved the extermination of *Kulaks* as a class in early 1930.

In December 1958, we finally came to America. I had relatives here who rented an apartment for us in Grand Concourse, in the Bronx. My daughters went to school in America even though they didn't know English yet, and I got a job as a nurse's aide in New York. I remarried in 1964, and we lived in Yorktown Heights, New York.

I thought I was not a lucky person, but I am lucky to have had my grandparents, two great people. My oldest daughter has two masters' degrees and is a Special Education teacher in Tucson. She came to Arizona with her husband, who was in the military and stationed at Fort Huachuca. They moved to Tucson after that. I came to Tucson in 2005. My second daughter is an office manager in New York. My grandson is a teacher with two masters degrees, and my other grandson works for the Lockheed Martin Corporation. A few years ago he put something into orbit. He graduated from Stanford.[9]

---

[9] Eva Siebert passed away on May 7, 2012.

Mary Sterina

Belarus

I was born on March 22, 1941, in Gomel, Belarus, three months before the war began. Because I was just three months old, everything I write comes from my mother, Lyubov Romanovna Ginzburg. She was a shift supervisor at a textile factory at the time and a member of the party.

In 1939 my mother's brother fell and was killed by a tram in Leningrad, leaving behind a wife and two young children. So my mother, who was on three months maternity leave, took in her brother's older child, five-year-old Ilyusha. Since my mother was involved in evacuating a factory to the Urals after the war began, me, Ilyusha, and my eleven-year-old brother Victor went with her.

The train moved slowly and made many long stops. There was nothing to eat. The children climbed along the platforms and on the wagons. Once, they found a whole barrel of anchovies, which was a real holiday! My mother ate anchovies, drank water, and breastfed me.

We arrived at Chkalov (now Orenburg) after several weeks travel. There, my mother turned over the equipment she had been put in charge of. A very nice older woman took us into her home on the outskirts of the city. Perhaps she wasn't so old, but that's how it seemed to me. We called her Anna Fedorovna. She would babysit me and let my mother go to work.

My mother's aunt and uncle found us and settled in as well. My mother left the knitting factory for a factory that made pasta, where she would sometimes glue dough to her stomach, bring it home, bake it and feed us bread. My uncle was a shoemaker and my aunt saved all his money, so when they returned to Gomel she bought a house that was a duplex with a large orchard. After they left, my mother gave Anna Fedorovna my stockings and asked her to sell them to buy bread for us. I ate poorly, even when food was available. My mother sought out her half-sister, Fenya, who arrived at our house wearing a dress made from a bag with three holes cut in it for her arms and head. She had a son three years older than me. She'd had a heart defect since she was a child, and my mother would not let her work. Only my mother worked.

My father returned after the war ended, where he'd been wounded. His real profession was tailoring, so he built a shop and we lived generally well. My brother graduated and applied for medical school when I was in the first grade. He was an excellent student and a Stalin Scholar. I was thin and feeble, and often sick.

My mother also cared for the disabled. She too care of a blind man who wanted to move to another city who demanded that the executive committee transfer his twelve-square-meter room to my mother. We now had our own home. But to return to Belarus was impossible because we had no money and there was nowhere to go there.

A college professor who taught the cello lived in an even larger room in our building. He'd once even taught Rostropovich. Nikolay Ivanovich, as we called him, treated us with such respect, and even offered to switch rooms with us. He lived alone, and my mother always tried to help him. This is the very room my parents exchanged in order to move to Minsk.[1] By this time I was nineteen years old and didn't live at home.

After I completed school, I went to Belarus and attended a commercial college. My parents returned while I was in my second year. Years after the war, in Orenburg, we read a newspaper article that described my mother's train trip to the Urals as a "feat," yet she never received an award. Even when she requested permission for a communist party food basket, she was denied. They said they'd do it when she was a party member for 50 years. She didn't live that long.

My father was terribly ill. He survived three heart attacks, but died when he had a fourth. My mother was alone. She became sick as well, and retired at 52 with a disability. My uncle's wife survived the blockade in Leningrad with her youngest son, and after the war reunited with her oldest son, Ilyusha. My older brother Victor became a respected surgeon. He died in February 2010, at the age of 80.

---

[1] In the Soviet Union, the only way to move from one home to another was through official exchanges with another family.

Miklós Szilágyi

Hungary

I was eight years old when they took my mother.[1] Just like that: two thugs
in green shirts came with a list of young women, gave them 10 minutes to
dress, and herded them to a brick factory. From there they were taken by
foot to a concentration camp in Austria. Along their 400-mile trek they
were beaten, abused, spat upon, and starved.

My mother was everything to me. She was young, beautiful, feminine,
with large brown eyes – and she was my mother. They took my father
much earlier, first in 1940 for forced labor and again in 1942, when he
was sent to a "Punishment Company," which meant he wouldn't return.
The men who were in charge of the Jewish "work servicemen" were told
that they would get a leave from the Army as soon as they managed to
"de-Jew" their units; i.e., murder all the people under their command.

When this became clear to her, my mother went to see Ferenc
Herczeg. He was the most famous official writer of Admiral Horthy's
regime. My father worked in the Great Writer's print shop and set all his
novels and magazines by hand. The Great Writer liked my father; he
autographed all his novels to "Mr. Szilágyi, the master of letters." He
agreed to see my mother, who begged him to save her husband. The
Great Writer looked at her in disbelief: "Madame, but your husband is a
Jew!"

I will never forget the night my father had to go. After he left, I lay in
bed close to my mother and couldn't sleep. I watched her breathing: "Oh
G-d, I'm only six years old, at least keep my mother with me!" Six
months later the wives of all "work servicemen" from my father's unit
received official notification: "Your husband has disappeared during

---

[1] This story is an excerpt from Miklós Szilágyi's book, *The Story of My Times*.

military action." The good soldiers managed to completely "de-Jew" their units—they had earned a vacation.

On March 19, 1944, the Germans formally occupied Hungary. Their first – and seemingly most important – task was to eliminate the Jews. They immediately sent Adolf Eichmann to Hungary, and established a puppet government with a special secretary for the "solution to the Jewish problem." They ordered all Jews to wear yellow stars on their clothes. At this point we became prey to anyone. We were treated like rats. It is very painful to remember how eagerly the Hungarian people cooperated with the Germans in rounding up all the Jews who lived outside Budapest, concentrating them first in ghettos, then packing them into boxcars designed to transport cattle (a hundred people in each car without food or water) and taking them to Auschwitz. Altogether, about 600,000 Hungarian Jews perished, including dozens of my relatives.

In June 1944, we were concentrated in specially designated houses all over the city. Each Jewish family was allowed to use one room. As most of the apartments in Budapest had more than one room each, the extra rooms were used to house those families who were evacuated from their homes. Designated Jewish houses were marked with huge yellow stars. The list of inhabitants was posted at the entrance to each house. The caretakers of these houses were personally responsible for "their yids." They went out of their way to comply. We could leave the house only during specially determined hours and had to report to the caretaker each time we left and when we returned. The caretaker's son served on the Russian front as a noncommissioned officer, and the proud father took every opportunity to express his dismay that while his son was occupied with the honored task of saving Hungary from the Bolsheviks, he had to deal with "you lousy, filthy yids."

The remaining days of school were torture. The kids now openly enjoyed themselves at our expense. They subjected us to constant abuse. Then we went home to the yellow-star house where the forced concentration of old people, women, and children led to a barrage of quarrels and arguments. We were allowed neither to visit anyone nor to have visitors. We were not allowed to enter public parks, and could use only the back coaches of the streetcars. We continued to spend our nights in the underground shelter, scared to death of the carpet bombings.

I badly needed a haircut, and we knew the nearby barber quite well; he had always cut my hair, and used to greet my mother with a great smile: "Let me kiss your hand, Madame Szilágyi!" This time he was a different man. When I entered his shop, he started to yell: "Filthy little yid, haven't you learned your Kol Nidrei yet?[2] Get out of here before I tear your long ears off!"

Time went by. On the evening of October 15, the radio suddenly stopped its regular programming. "We shall now broadcast the special proclamation of our Regent, Admiral Miklós Horthy of Nagybánya," said the announcer. We all froze in awe; we knew history was being made at this moment. In his proclamation the Admiral declared that Germany was losing the war and he had decided to break with Hitler and join the allies to finish the war as soon as possible. We were sitting in front of the radio, hardly believing what we were hearing. Then suddenly, the joy of freedom overwhelmed us, and we started to remove the yellow stars from our clothes. "Wait," said my grandfather, "it's not over yet." Unfortunately, as always, he was right.

A couple of hours later the radio broadcast a new announcement. The Admiral was deposed by the Germans, taken into custody, and the Arrow Cross Party took over leadership of the country.[3] This was the most terrible thing that could possibly happen to Hungary, and especially to us. The Arrow Cross Party was a bunch of failed people. Their leader, Ferenc Szálasi, was a failed army officer who later also failed as a journalist. Their second-in-command made his living as a corn-cutter because he failed in everything else. These people called each other "Brothers".

The "Brothers" decided to deport as many of the remaining Jews from Budapest as they could to the death camps, but they must have realized, as the Soviet Red Army was approaching the capital, that they had to find a solution within the city. They decided to designate a ghetto in the middle of the city and eliminate the leftover Jewish population right there.

---

[2] Prayer recited at the beginning of the evening service on Yom Kippur.
[3] The Arrow Cross Party, Hungary's national socialist party, led the nation from October 1944 to March 1945. The party was ruthlessly anti-Semitic.

My teeth chattered in horror. That night I begged my mother: "Please, please mommy, tuck me into bed and stay with me. Please, don't go to sleep, I'm so scared!"

They came to take my mother a few days later. She just looked at me with her beautiful big eyes . . . and went away. I couldn't even cry.

My grandfather and I were now alone. My grandfather was a respected man who used to work for the Hungarian State Railroad, but as a young man he was an elementary school teacher. My grandmother died early, and my grandfather raised his four children alone. His youngest son was lucky to die of pneumonia at the age of 16 in 1939, but his other two sons, and now his daughter, were taken away from him by force. He couldn't cope with all of this. He was a broken man, a mere shadow of his former self. But he still had to take care of me, and this gave him some strength.

The "Brothers" came for us on November 27, 1944. First they ordered us to collect all our belongings, except glassware and furniture, and throw everything down from the staircase onto the inner courtyard of the house.

The "Brothers" were supposed to decide who to take to the brick factory and who to take to the ghetto. It seemed obvious to everyone that the ghetto was a better choice: we thought that it was only a matter of days before the Red Army would enter Budapest and save our lives. The brick factory meant a death walk to the gas chamber at a remote concentration camp far from the front. Therefore, when my grandfather and I were both ordered to stand with the group designated for the brick factory, we knew our days were numbered. A little discussion among the "Brothers," however, occurred: the brick factory was far away and none of them wanted to go there. After some ten minutes of quarreling, the chief "Brother" announced his decision: "We'll take the whole rabble of filthy yids to the ghetto."

We were allowed to take as much as we could carry. All our belongings that we'd previously thrown down were taken away in a big truck, and we never saw them again. We were ordered to form a double line and walk toward the inner city. We joined groups of Jews from other yellow-star houses who were also marched in the same direction. Finally, the small streams formed a big river of people all marching toward the ghetto. As we marched, the "Brothers" yelled at us, kicked us, spat at us, and shot randomly into the crowd. They immensely enjoyed being the unquestioned masters of so many innocent people (as it turned out later, approximately 80,000 people were taken to the ghetto that day). The people on the street looked at us, laughed, and made rude comments such as "Look how upset the stinking yids are," and "Finally they'll find the place where they belong." I did not see a single sympathetic or concerned face in the crowd.

One old man from our house had terminal cancer, and could not walk any longer. They shot him a couple of feet from me, and kicked his body aside. His wife tried to stay with him, but they forced her back into the marching column. As we approached the inner city, the shootings became increasingly frequent. Finally, we were walking in a thick mess of blood. "What is this under our feet?" I asked my grandfather. "Oil," he answered after some hesitation.

It was late afternoon when we arrived at a big square named Klauzál tér. The square was full of Jews. We were surrounded by the Arrow Cross "Brothers," who by now had lost every trace of humanity that they might have had left. "Brother, don't you see how difficult it is for this Jewish woman to carry her bag?" asked one of them. "Indeed," replied the other, "I must help her!" And he shot the Jewish woman twice in the head. Another came to an old man and said: "Why do you carry your bag? Don't you understand that you won't need anything in a very short time?"

As if to confirm this statement, the loudspeaker announced: "At this time you are ordered to drop into the designated containers all money, jewelry, watches, and any other valuable items you might have. You will be searched afterwards. If any valuables are found on you, you will be hacked to pieces on the spot." My grandfather went to one of the containers and dropped all his money and valuables into it . . . except for one thing. He carried my grandmother's old golden pocket watch, his only tangible memory from his deceased wife. The watch was a masterpiece. My grandmother received it from her grandmother as a wedding present in 1909. I saw that my grandfather "forgot" about the watch and whispered into his ear not to risk his life, but he had evidently made up his mind.

My blood froze when I saw an Arrow Cross "Brother" approaching my grandfather. He was about fourteen years old, with an automatic weapon in his hand. The lust for blood was evident in his colorless eyes. I wanted to ask him, "How many people have you killed today?" but I was too scared to open my mouth. He searched my grandfather and immediately found the watch. He took him aside to shoot him. I was crying desperately and praying for my grandfather's life. Then something unexpected happened. The young lad evidently recognized that the watch was valuable, and changed his mind. "You will be hacked to pieces on the spot!" he hissed at my grandfather, and dropped the watch into his own pocket as he walked away.

It was already late evening when we arrived in the ghetto. It was a relatively small area of the inner city, previously inhabited mostly by Jews. The Arrow Cross Party ordered all non-Jewish tenants out of their homes with the promise that after the yids were taken care of, they could return and would be rewarded. Several hundred of us were distributed to each building. Inside the house, we were divided into apartments. The apartment we were ordered into formerly belonged to a religious Jewish family. There was nothing left in it except for furniture, glassware, and some old photographs. 21 of us had to sleep in each room. Of course, there were only a couple of beds in the room, and no sheets. We lay down on the floor, exhausted, depressed, and without hope. Nobody slept that night.

There was nothing for us to eat. They didn't bring us there to eat. The only source of food was that organized by the so-called Jewish Council, which tried to take care of the internal matters of the ghetto. They were somehow able to smuggle some food in; occasionally, they could get some soup for the children. The most frequent cause of death was starvation. After December 10, 1944, when the gates of the ghetto were sealed, there was no more food from the outside. Then dying of hunger became a commonplace event. It started with diarrhea, and mental disorder followed. In their final days the victims talked only about food. They died imagining themselves sitting in a fashionable café in sunlit pre-war Budapest and eating the best strudels in Central Europe.

As the front was approaching Budapest, the Arrow Cross Party decided to seal the ghetto off. Before the gates were closed, they allowed the non-Jewish former inhabitants to visit for the last time. I then experienced a most unexpected encounter. I had already witnessed people being shot and dying of hunger, but the following little conversation surpassed everything. It remains vivid to this day, and took place between the former janitor of the house and my grandfather. The middle-aged woman suddenly burst into tears, and became hysterical. My grandfather tried to comfort her, but she was desperate. She said: "they have ruined my life! Don't you understand, they will blow you up, and *I'll lose all my furniture!*"

After a rumor was spread that everybody over 60 would be shot, my grandfather had a strange idea. He declared that he would walk out of the ghetto and visit the Pension Office of the Hungarian Railroads to complain that they'd failed to deliver his pension for the past two months. I remembered the incident of my grandmother's watch too well; I tried to persuade my grandfather that this was the equivalent to suicide, but, again, he had already made up his mind. It was a cold morning; he put on his warm coat and fur hat and walked towards the gate. I followed him, crying. "You lousy old yid, where do you think you are going?" asked the Arrow Cross guard at the gate. "I am going to get my pension," said my grandfather. The guard burst into laughter: "Did you hear the old yid, Brothers? He's gonna get his pension!" With this, he raised his rifle high in the air and crashed it down on my grandfather's head with the stock of his rifle, using all his strength. The old man's body spun around several times before falling down. I tried to drag him back as fast as I could. I pulled him inside a house. People came to help, and it turned out that G-d had saved him a second time: the fur hat took most of the blow, and he escaped with bruises and a temporary loss of consciousness.

On Christmas Eve the ring was closed around the city. The siege of Budapest began. The whistles of bombs and shells became the music of the day: they brought destruction and fear, but also the hope that the end of our sufferings was near. Now we permanently moved underground. The cellar was overcrowded, there was absolutely nothing to eat, and water was scarce. People were dying like flies, and soon everyone was covered with lice.

It was forbidden to practice our religion "by penalty of

dismemberment." Nevertheless, when the time of Hanukkah came, an old Rabbi climbed through the underground cellars from house to house and delivered the holiday service. We were sitting there, starving, lousy Jews and when we cried out "Yevareheho Adonai eleiho," the whole shelter became a monolithic sobbing mass of doomed people who were finally at peace with themselves and ready to die.

Many of us did die. I will never forget the eyes of the middle-aged lady who died of hunger one day before the liberation of the ghetto. Then I was already delirious; I'd eaten absolutely nothing for the last nine days. The next morning, on January 18, 1945, the Russians were suddenly there. No more Arrow Cross, no more Germans, just tired, dirty, and drunken Russian soldiers who smiled at us and tore the yellow stars off our clothes.

And they gave us food. A truck came with bread, and a huge crowd of starving people surrounded it immediately. A Russian soldier stood on top of the truck and threw loaves of bread into the crowd. My grandfather came back, barely alive, with two loaves of fresh bread wrapped in his old white scarf, which was covered with lice.

Then people started to eat. They ate like animals, stuffing the fresh bread into their mouths, swallowing without chewing, filling their empty stomachs. Many of them paid with their lives for their hunger reflex: their exhausted intestines couldn't deal with so much food in such a short time, and they died. Fortunately, my grandfather knew this: he cut one piece of bread for me and one for himself. I happily ate the bread and was grateful to G-d that I was alive.

At about 10 o'clock in the morning my grandfather told me: "Although we are both very weak, we must leave this place immediately." We left and headed home. The one-mile walk took us the whole day. There were no streets, just ruins. The bodies of dead people and dead horses covered the whole city. But the war was far from over. The Germans still held Buda (the hilly part of the city on the western side of the Danube), and they were shooting over the river with their artillery. One of my grandfather's sisters and her daughter were killed several days later by these shells.

We finally arrived home. Our neighbors greeted us as if we were just back from a short vacation. No apologies, no shame, nothing. They gave us some food, however, and we climbed the stairs to find our apartment empty. There was some furniture left but no clothes and no windows and it was a very cold winter. My grandfather found some blankets and some paper to light fire in the stove. We went down to the street and brought a couple of bricks to heat up and keep us warm for the night.

The next day we found out that not all of our problems had been solved by staying alive. The Russians did not come to save the lives of the Jews (although they did save ours!) but to establish their empire. Accordingly, they were seeking men to take them "for a little work," which meant dozens of years in the Gulag. The Arrow Cross brothers quickly understood how to avoid this and use it for new opportunities at the same time. The other side of their armbands happened to be red, so they turned the bands inside out and immediately became activists of the newly formed Hungarian Communist Party.

There were still no utilities and little food in the city. Although surrounded by the Red Army, the Germans continued to hold Buda for almost a month. They even managed to push the front back, and almost took the whole capital again. They mercilessly destroyed this beautiful city, "the pearl of the Danube," and blew up all of our bridges when they retreated to Buda.

We had no money, nothing. My grandfather found two small tin bowls and two canteens, took me by the hand, and we went around panhandling. Wherever we found a place where some food was being sold, the old man swallowed his pride and begged: "Please, give something to this child." And they did. Sometimes they even gave my grandfather something to eat, but he always shared his part with me.

As my grandfather's health began to deteriorate, we both came to the conclusion that I could not remain with him much longer. There was a new organization called National Salvation that had a program to take the hungry children of Budapest to the villages and have them work there for food. So I bid farewell to my grandfather and went to Orosháza, a small town approximately 150 miles southeast of Budapest. The peasants already knew about our arrival and were eagerly looking forward to the free labor force. Since I was so skinny – all my bones could be seen through my skin – nobody wanted to take me. Finally, the officials of the National Salvation virtually forced an old, poor, and blind couple to take me in. They reluctantly agreed on the condition that I help them all the time, and not attend school.

It was already March and I hadn't been to school since the previous summer. I was thirsty for knowledge, and couldn't accept that condition. A couple of days later I escaped. I was nine-years old and alone in the world. But this is another story.

Manya Tepelboym

Ukraine

I am Manya Tepelboym, born into a Jewish family on December 31, 1928, in Proskurov (now Khmelnitsky), Ukraine. My mother was a housewife and my father was a tinsmith. I was twelve years old when the war began in June 1941.

My parents decided to evacuate from Ukraine, but we were unable to get on one of the trains leaving. On July 23, when the Germans had approached Proskurov, we ran from the city and stayed overnight in a house in a large village near the regional center of Derazhnya. The owner was nice. He woke us in the middle of the night and said the Germans were approaching Derazhnya. A nearby home was burning, and he said the people who lived there had set the fire themselves to keep the Germans back. He gave us a horse and a wagon, and thanks to that we were saved.

We arrived at a river with a bridge that was so overloaded with retreating troops that we couldn't use it. One of the soldiers told us how to get to a nearby pontoon bridge and that they were going to blow up the main bridge once the troops crossed it. We crossed the river on the pontoon bridge, along with others fleeing, and entered the woods. We ran through the woods as German aircraft strafed us, and many people were killed. Leaving the woods, we continued to run. Near Vinnitsa, Ukraine, German pilots again strafed us from low level. I can still remember their faces as they fired at us. It was horrible. We only survived after hiding near a hill on the bank of a river. We continued on after the aircraft flew away. There were dead bodies everywhere and not many survivors.

We made it to Zolotonosha, where it was quiet. The station master there said the city had not been bombed. We boarded a train headed for

Poltava, but the train stopped at Lozovaya station. All the trains had stopped. On the fourth day we caught another train.

Our ordeal is difficult to describe. My father was not well (which kept him from being drafted into the army) and could hardly stand. We finally started feeling better once we were able to get on a train. The train was heading across Russia and had stopped at Tashkent, Uzbekistan. My father died there, at the station, and my mother and I were left alone. We were taken from an evacuation center to a distant Uzbeki village, where the villagers didn't like evacuees. We tried to buy food but they wouldn't sell us anything. My mother was afraid they would kill us, and decided that we should return. We went to Saratov, where they asked her where we were going. She answered, "Ukraine," but we hadn't heard that Ukraine and part of Russia were then controlled by the Germans. We returned to the evacuation center.

From there we were taken to the Baranovka Atkarsky area in the Saratov region of Russia. We lived two-and-a-half years there, and I worked on a collective farm. My mother was sick the entire time and couldn't work. I remember that I went hungry the whole time.

We returned home to Proskurov in June 1944, just after it had been liberated. There was a large crater where our house had been, and when my mother saw it she became sick. We found out that all of our relatives –18 people – had been killed. The Germans had shot all the Jews in the woods. These fascist monsters had not spared anyone, not even the elderly or the children. City authorities provided us with a room, and I went to school. My mother couldn't work because of her health. I started working in 1945. I had studied to be a bookkeeper and at the same time graduated from school.

In 1991 my son, his wife, and I decided to go to America after being invited by one of our relatives. We had several reasons to leave. For one, there was anti-Semitism in the Soviet Union, even in positions of power, which everyone knew. A second reason was that my son was not well. He suffered two heart attacks in Kiev and needed surgery, which was performed in America. So we found ourselves here, in Tucson, Arizona, where there's a Holocaust Survivor program. The program helps me and supports me. I am very thankful for that.

Mirjam Wheeler

Czechoslovakia

I was born in August of either 1936 or 1937, in a very small village in Czechoslovakia called Kurima. I don't know the exact year, or even date in August I was born, but it was either August 18 or 23. Our village was primitive, without plumbing or electricity, but it was nice. My father and his brother married two cousins, and we all lived together with my grandparents there. I think my father's name was Ernst Stern, but I'm not sure. I think my mother's name was Elenor. I had an older sister, but she died before the Holocaust. My sister Judith survived the Holocaust too, but my brother was found hiding in the woods and was killed. He was eight or nine years old at the time.

I think I was five years old when our parents sent us to Hungary to live with my aunt. They divided us children up to make sure that if anyone was captured it wouldn't be all of us. My cousins and me were caught crossing into Hungary, and I remember being in prison. We had to go to a horrible orphanage for about a year instead of staying with my aunt, but we could at least visit her. My sister made it, but when the Germans entered Hungary we were smuggled back to Czechoslovakia. This was the last time I saw my parents. According to my sister, who wrote a book about the Holocaust, we were only home for about two hours.[1] My father arranged for us to be hidden in different places.

My sister and I stayed with a Catholic couple, in their back room. We couldn't have the lights on, and we couldn't go outside. But one of the neighbors betrayed us and called the Gestapo. In the middle of the night, three trucks of German soldiers with guns and dogs came just to capture

---

[1] Ms. Wheeler's sister's book is: *Say the Name: A Survivor's Tale in Prose and Poetry*, by Judith H. Sherman (University of New Mexico Press, 2005).

my thirteen-year-old sister and me. I was six at the time. I think they did these kinds of things just to scare people.

I was put in a Gestapo prison, an old castle on a hill. I don't know how long I was there, but they kept asking me where my parents were and where other Jews were. My parents had been very smart and had never believed what Hitler said. They also hadn't told us anything, because they knew it would be dangerous. We really didn't know anything. The Germans would try to bribe me with chocolate to tell them.

One night a Czechoslovakian guard came and told us to follow him. He led us out of the prison, which was a real miracle because people didn't generally get out of Gestapo prisons. My sister went into the forest with a group of people and I went into hiding with another family. They eventually caught my sister; she ended up in Ravensbrück.[2] The husband in the family that hid me was anti-Nazi, so he was in hiding too. They didn't realize what was involved in hiding me, and that they could have all been shot. They had four children.

Eventually, the family also had German soldiers living downstairs, even while I was hiding upstairs. The Germans were always looking for the father, meaning they could find me as they searched. The woman got very scared about this. All this caused fights between the couple, because the woman wanted to give me up. But he wouldn't let her. She didn't do it, but she'd always tell me horror stories about what the Germans would do so I'd stay quiet. It was very scary thinking that they could find me.

While I was there I got very sick and the couple didn't know what to do. There was a Jewish doctor in hiding in the area, but they couldn't get him, so another doctor came – I think a German doctor – who gave me medication. I recovered eventually, but the woman was always so worried. She didn't know what to do. I'd call for water but she couldn't think to even take care of me. All I knew was that if I didn't call for water I'd disappear. I'd hear her talking to her daughters, saying things like, "How are we going to bury her? She's not supposed to be here!" But here I am.

---

[2] Ravensbrück concentration camp primarily housed female prisoners, approximately 50,000 of whom died from disease, starvation, and overwork, and 2,200 were killed in gas chambers. The camp was liberated on April 30, 1945.

My parents must have told everyone where we were hiding, because when the war ended my cousins came for me. We all went back to my house in the village to wait for whoever else might come home. Our parents didn't. My brother and grandparents didn't. But my two cousins and my sister and I did come back. As it turned out, my father and his brother were sent to Sachsenhausen concentration camp, where his brother died just before the war ended.[3] My father died there the week after the war ended. My mother was supposed to be sent to a concentration camp, but she became ill. My sister and aunt went to see her, without papers, and a woman on the train gave my sister fruit and bread. My sister didn't know the blessing, so she told the woman she'd wait until my aunt woke up. It was a miracle that there were no soldiers onboard. My sister got to see my mother one last time before she passed away.

We lived with my aunt for a year, and we just barely got out of Czechoslovakia before the Russians closed all the borders. After that you couldn't get out until 1958 or so. We went to England, because the English were willing to take 1,500 children. However, they could only find around 700, because small children had been put to death right away. The place in England where we lived was wonderful.

I was in England for 14 years or so, and my sister and cousin had gone to America after they got married. I joined them later, but even though we were British citizens at that point, I had to go to America as part of the quota of Czechoslovakians visas. So I had to wait four years. I arrived in America in the late 1950s and lived with my family in New Jersey for a year, then moved to Manhattan until I moved to California. I moved to Sierra Vista, Arizona, 10 years ago.

Some things about the war are vague to me, because I was pretty young. But it was very hard to be all by myself back then, and the houses had to stay dark all the time when the people hiding me left. The Gestapo usually came at night, and one time the woman I was staying

---

[3] Sachsenhausen was a concentration camp in Oranienburg, Germany where approximately 30,000 inmates died from exhaustion, disease, malnutrition and sickness. Many were executed or died as the result of brutal medical experiments.

with pushed me under her bed. No one was sure if they'd find me.

There was something really good that happened from all of this: when I lived in New York I would write to the family that hid me. They told me the father was very ill and that they couldn't get medication for him, so we were able to get the medication through the Red Cross in Holland. He lived another three years after that. I didn't keep too much contact with them after that, because I don't know Czechoslovakian anymore. Still, that made me feel good.

Wanda Wolosky

Poland

Of course my mother knew about the war.[1] It was in all the newspapers, but nobody discussed the war with me. I probably wouldn't have understood. My father and his brother Henry decided to go to Russia. Russia was not at war with Germany at that time. One morning I woke up, and I was all alone in the apartment.[2] I heard planes flying over the city and bombs falling. I went to the window and looked out onto the street. The street was a blanket of white down feathers that had come from pillows and blankets. A house was struck by a bomb. One house on the street was in ruins and another was on fire. I could see people in the street, running and screaming. I didn't know what was happening. The bombing went on for a month and there was chaos in the city.

Starvation began to hit the city shortly after the first bombing raids. There were bread lines, and there were shortages of water because the Germans had bombed the water pipes. My mother was well known at the bakery across the street from our house, so she was able to get bread for a while. However, the bakery soon ran out of flour. I cried for days because I was so hungry. My mother could do nothing to ease my hunger. The German planes were flying ceaselessly. Even in the basement you could hear the sounds of the bombs hitting. If the hit was close, the basement shook. People were praying, hoping this was not their last day on earth.

The Germans marched into Warsaw in the beginning of October 1939. Trucks full of solders and motorcycles. Everything was motorized.

---

[1] This story is an excerpt from Wanda Wolosky's book, *After All: Life Can Be Beautiful*.

[2] Ms. Wolosky was born and raised in Warsaw, Poland, where she was living when World War II began.

Not a smile on their faces. The occupation had started. I was five years old. The occupiers immediately began to give decrees. They figured that all the people had lice, so their first order was for everyone to be deloused. I went with my mother to the place we were assigned to. It was in a basement of a building. They told us to undress and then sprayed us with DDT, which is a toxic substance that is no longer used because it is so hazardous.

There were new orders all the time. Jews could only have 2,000 zloty in the bank, and could only withdraw 200 zloty per week to feed their families. Another order came making it illegal for Jewish doctors to practice on Aryan patients. Teachers couldn't teach any more. If you had a business, you had to give it up. No work, no money; true starvation had begun.

The Germans went to Jewish homes to confiscate furniture, household appliances, paintings and valuables. If you tried to resist, they would punish you. They tortured babies, and beat pregnant women and the elderly. No one was safe at home or on the streets. Jewish women were publicly humiliated, forced to undress in the street and undergo body searches. The Germans took their jewelry and fur coats, and abused them sexually. If you tried to protest, you were beaten. They searched women's breasts and their private body parts, forcing husbands and children to watch.

There was another order from the Germans: this time they wanted all of the Jews who lived in different parts of the city to be moved into one designated section of the city, "The Ghetto," to keep them all together. My mother was lucky: she was able to exchange our apartment with an Aryan family's apartment in the section that was designated for the Ghetto, on Nowolipki Street. She did this quickly; she didn't wait until the last minute. The apartment was small, with only enough space to fit three single beds side-by-side, but that was fine. My grandmother was able to get a place for her and Zeilek in the same building.[3] She was sharing her place with others. We were happy because we were close together. We did have some time to move some of our belongings, and took whatever we could carry.

---

[3] Zeilek is Ms. Wolosky's uncle.

Jews were not allowed to have American dollars, but we got a letter from my father's mother, my Grandmother Rose, who was living in the United States, saying that she was sending us money. In order to get our money, we had to leave the Ghetto. There was a tram that went through the streets of the Ghetto to the Aryan side of Warsaw. My mother and I dressed nicely, and when the tram came through the Ghetto we jumped on it. Nobody said anything to us. My mother had to wear an arm band with the Jewish star, but I didn't have to, as the rule didn't apply to children under the age of twelve (in Warsaw). She took it off and put it in her pocket. We went to the bank on the Aryan side, hoping all the way that we would be successful in getting the money out. When we got there, the tellers stared at us but said nothing, and gave us our money. That was a miracle. We jumped on the tram, and arrived back at the Ghetto.

The Germans decided that it wasn't enough just to have all the Jews in one section of the city. They decided that the Jews needed to build a wall around the Ghetto, and that they had to pay for it themselves. So the Jews built the wall, which included gates. The wall was very tall, and as an extra precaution, to prevent people from trying to climb over it and get out, they put broken glass on the top of it. The gate was guarded by German soldiers, Polish police, and Jewish police. The Germans recruited Jewish people, some of whom were not very nice.

A Jewish committee was formed in the Ghetto. One of their jobs was to place as many people as possible in each room. Even so, there was not going to be enough room for half a million people in an area designated for two hundred and fifty thousand people. A Jewish policeman was assigned to live with us in our apartment. He was a good guy, and provided us with some useful information.

Starvation quickly started in the Ghetto. The daily calorie intake per person was 184, which was a slice of bread and watery soup. It was the Jewish committee that organized the soup kitchens. Children suffered the most. They walked around looking like living skeletons. Some lay on the sidewalks, looking at us with big, empty eyes. Their ragged clothes hung over their skeletal bodies. They were skin and bones.

The food situation was getting worse and worse. My mother and I became smugglers. If you got caught smuggling you were shot on the spot. There were a few different methods for leaving the Ghetto. When we heard a rumor that there was a hole in the wall or tunnel from the Ghetto to the Aryan side, we would get out that way. Another way was to go through the sewage system. Many other times we would stand by the gate and wait for a good German to let us pass. Some of the Germans had a heart, but not too many. Polish winters were extremely cold and we could wait for hours for a good German. I would shake, almost frozen, and cry from the cold and exhaustion.

Leaving the ghetto became more and more challenging to do. One day a Polish friend of ours came to see us. He was a foreman in one of the factories that had been established in the Ghetto. He said to my mother: "Blima, I am going to take your daughter with me, and tomorrow I'm going to bring her back with food." So that day he took me with him after work. I don't remember his name, and I don't remember exactly where his home was. In the morning he cut a big chunk from the belly of a dead pig and wrapped it around my body under my arms. It was very tight. I walked with him back to the gates of the Ghetto. The German guard at the gate asked him for his pass. After examining the pass and seeing that all was in order, the guard returned his papers to him. Then he looked at me, put his hand on my shoulder, and said, "Are you cold my child?" I was sweating from every pore of my body because if his hand had touched just a little lower than my shoulder, he would have felt the meat that was wrapped around my body, under my coat. Instead of hearing "frierst du mein kin" (are you cold my child), I would have felt a bullet shoot through my head. The food we received lasted for quite some time.

Curfew was at 7 p.m. If you got caught on the street after curfew, you were shot. Not far from us was a prison by the name of Pawiak. The Germans used to pick up people in the street or pull them from their houses and take them to Pawiak. If you went to Pawiak you almost never came out alive. I know of only one person who ever came out alive. Her name was Irena Sandler. She was a Polish social worker who saved more than 2,500 children by smuggling them out of the Ghetto. She was eventually caught by the Germans, tortured, and was supposed to be executed, but the Polish underground bribed a German to let her escape. She died when she was in her 90s. At night, I could hear shooting come from Pawiak.

When an SS officer came into the Ghetto, he expected to have the entire sidewalk to himself. One day I was walking with my mother and there was an SS officer walking on the other side of the street. A small child on the same side of the street as this SS officer did not have enough time to get out of his way, so he picked the child up by his feet and bashed his head against the wall. He dropped the dead child's body in the gutter. You would walk down the street and there were dead bodies lying around. You did not pay attention; it was a daily occurrence. Tomorrow it might be you.

The smell of death was everywhere. A group of undertakers would be picking up the dead bodies and throwing them on a cart. There were times when there was not enough time to pick up all the bodies, so they would lie in the streets for a day or more. Sickness took hold of the Ghetto. There was rampant malnutrition, tuberculosis, and typhus because of the lice. Life was cheap in the Ghetto; it had little value.

The Germans were ordering 6,000 people to report to the railroad station every day. They said these people were being relocated. No one knew where the trains were going. The Jewish police would round up people to be shipped out.

We hated living in the Ghetto. This was not living. So one day when we left the ghetto, my mother said we were not going back. We took absolutely nothing with us. All we had were the clothes on our backs. We slept for a few days under the steps of buildings and in basements. One day while we were walking we saw the woman from our old apartment building. This woman hated Jews and us. At one time my mother gave her a loaf of bread. That loaf of bread changed her around. My mother told her we were looking for a place to stay. There was a small building in the cemetery where she was working. She took us there and stayed with us during the day for a few weeks, bringing food and sharing it with us. We couldn't use the stove for heat at night and it was freezing cold. The smoke would have given away the fact that somebody was staying in the cemetery at night. We could only have a fire during daylight hours. After some time my mother found another place for us, which happened to be very close to the Ghetto.

It was April 1943 when the fighting in the Ghetto started. Inside the Ghetto, young people decided that if they were going to die, they would rather die fighting than go like sheep. They bought some guns from the Polish underground, and were able to obtain some uniforms from a factory inside the Ghetto where German uniforms were made. There was a rumor that some of the young people who spoke German would disguise themselves in German uniforms. They would point out a building to the Germans and tell them that there were Jews hiding there. The Germans would go to the building, and the Jews would ambush them and take their guns. The Germans sent tanks to the Ghetto and then they went from house to house, capturing and killing everybody. At night we could see from where we were staying that the sky over the Ghetto was all red. The Ghetto was burning.

The fighting lasted for one month and then the Ghetto no longer existed. The Germans gave another order that if a Jew was found hiding in any of the buildings, everyone would get shot. We left and started looking for yet another place to hide.

Note: Wanda survived in hiding until 1945, when the Russians liberated Poland. She and her mother were able to leave Poland for Israel in 1950, where Wanda took the Hebrew name Tova, which means "good". She served in the Israeli Army until 1954, and in 1957 she left Israel, eventually making her way to the United States. She married Gerry in 1958, and after their children were older the family moved back to Israel. They returned to the United States a few years later. When Gerry and Wanda retired, they moved to Green Valley, Arizona.

Valentina Yakorevskaya

Belarus

I was born on September 19, 1938, so I was just two years old when the war began. My memories of the start of the war, the evacuation from Belarus, and the first few years during the evacuation are therefore hazy and broken. Individual moments are separate and have stayed in my mind ever since. They're very clear. I'm writing these memories from discussions with my mother, Fira Yakovlevna Tamarkina.

When the war began my mother, father, younger sister and I lived in Mozyr, in the Gomel region (then known as Polesia) of Belarus. My sister Lyudmila was born on April 7, 1941, and was only two months old at the time. The Germans bombed Mozyr in the first days of the war, and there were already refugees from Brest all over the city. It was terrible. My father and others from the military committee captured German paratroopers. Several days after the war began, my father was sent to the front.

On July 1, 1941, my mother, little sister and me were evacuated from Mozyr. Despite my age at the time, I remember the day we evacuated. A large number of people were crying and screaming near a three-ton truck in which a man with a light-blue shirt (I remember the shirt color and how the man waved his arms) spoke loudly through a megaphone, gesturing.

My mother was able to take a suitcase with cloth diapers and baby things, and another suitcase with some clothing. All of our property was left behind. We were evacuated in freight cars filled with people, taking our places in upper-level seats. My mother dried cloth diapers on the seats, though there was nowhere to wash them. The Germans bombed the train as we traveled, and one bomb hit a car that burned. When they bombed us everyone would scatter from the cars and fall to the ground.

Although my mother had a baby, my sister, her breast milk had dried up, so when military trains stopped at the stations she'd ask the soldiers for any sort of produce: sugar, bread, and the foot wrappings they wore for socks to use for diapers. No one ever turned her down. The train didn't pass through Moscow, but went instead to a small town in the Stalingrad region called Chernyshka. My mother got a job teaching math at Basakino School there.

When the Germans began their offensive at Stalingrad we evacuated again. We lived with a Cossack woman in the village of Basakino. She tried to persuade my mother to leave my little sister, Mila, there with her. She said it would save Mila, but my mother refused and our journey continued.

A large tractor-pulled wagon stopped for us, but we went just a few dozen kilometers before the tractor ran out of gas. My mother stood on the side of the road with us while cattle from a nearby collective farm passed by, and finally persuaded the man driving the cattle to take us with him. They hitched an ox to the wagon and my mother drove the cart. The sun beat down on us mercilessly while we moved behind the herd. It was very dry. The clouds of dust were so thick that it seemed almost dark. Our eyes began to fester, and we ended up with boils and lice.

We made it to the Volga River, where all-day bombings had turned the place into sheer hell. Very many people were killed or drowned on boats or ferries heading for the opposite shore, but by some miracle we escaped injury and crossed. Refugees gathered at the train station there, and were taken away from the constant bombing to be put on freight trains. When our train stopped at stations for water, my mother would leave the car and run to the nearest house to ask for small amounts of bread, milk, and food for the children. She absolutely looked Jewish, but no one ever told her no. We were filthy, covered with lice, and constantly sick from malnutrition.

The train made it to the city of Zlatoust, in the Chelyabinsk region of the Urals, a transfer center for the evacuation. Dozens of trains arrived with evacuees who were then sent through cities in the Urals and further on to Siberia. In Zlatoust my mother joined up with her mother, my grandmother Lyubov Isakovna Tamarkin.

Zlatoust was a terrible city with awful, angry people. No one would help us. Residents would send out their dogs when a refugee knocked on their house gates. My mother and grandmother were robbed at the Zlatoust train station when they went to receive our scheduled train date. We were to go to the village of Chesna, in the Chelyabinsk region, where my mother was going to teach school. All we had left was a suitcase full of cloth diapers.

We made it to Chesna hungry, dirty, sick and out of clothes. But we did receive an apartment there. Many people were evacuees from Leningrad and from a Leningrad orphanage. The attitude toward evacuees was better in Chesna, but there was little help for us. We were very, very hungry. They fed us at preschool, but it wasn't enough. We were always hungry.

My personal recollections of that time were such: in the evening, when our landlord came home from work, she would prepare some food on the *pechka*, often boiled potatoes.[1] I would take my sister Mila to sit at the table, and we'd stare at our landlord with hungry eyes, waiting and wondering whether she'd give us food. My mother would yell at us to go to our room, but nothing helped. We would sit and wait, as if we were glued to our chairs.

But we always got something. I even remember the woman's name: Klava. She was very compassionate and felt sorry for us. There was no salt, and we got very little bread as there was almost none available. I think my sister and I picked up illnesses that we have had our whole lives from those terrible years of evacuation.

Something else occurred that I must say here: the leader of Chesna's communist party invited my mother to a party once. My mother went, and saw the party leader throw a piece of chocolate to his dog. My mother nearly fainted!

My father was killed on August 15, 1944, on the second Ukrainian front. There were many children like us in Chesna, kids whose fathers had been killed in the war. But there were two girls whose fathers sent them packages from the front. They were such well-dressed girls! And the

---

[1] A *pechka* was an oven that doubled as a furnace. In many cases people could sleep on them to keep warm in winter as well.

rest of us village children didn't like them.

It was very cold in the school where my mother worked. The teachers, mainly women, would stock up on wood for heating. We were all constantly sick. Though my mother received notification that my father had been killed, the joy we all felt on Victory Day was immeasurable. Almost everyone was crying from happiness, though many of the women were widows with small children to care for.

In 1945 we returned to Belarus after my mother was assigned to teach at Radoshkovichy School in Molodechno region. In Radoshkovichy, after the war, we also went hungry and were poorly housed. I attended school in Radoshkovichy up to the seventh grade.

My mother never spoke to us about anti-Semitism during those years, but I recall conversations from that time, so I know she constantly worried whether she would get the complete teacher's rate of pay with a few extra hours. She had two daughters and her mother on her hands. She alone had to feed the family. She was a widow at 30, and was beautiful and smart. But she didn't want to marry a second time. She was afraid that a husband would somehow reproach her children. I very well recall the conversations between my mother and grandmother about the fact that she was being stifled at the school, that the school director and the director of studies treated her unfairly. My mother taught physics and mathematics to seniors. She was a mathematician "from G-d."

We moved to Postava in 1952, where my mother also taught school. My sister and I finished our schooling there. My mother lived in Postava until 2009 – it became her home.

I graduated from Belarus State Institute of National Economics in 1955 in industrial economics. Because I graduated with a Red Diploma, I was assigned to work in a semi-closed optics factory in Minsk.[2] This was where I personally encountered anti-Semitism. In the human resources department, I had to provide my last name, first name, patronymic, and my mother's nationality.[3] My mother, Fira Yakovlevna Tamarkina, was Jewish. I used my father's last name, Zelenkovskaya, and although the

---

[2] A Red Diploma in the Soviet Union was awarded to top students. It's equivalent to graduating cum laude.

[3] Block Five of the Soviet passport indicated nationality. Soviet Jews were required to use "Jewish" in this nationality block.

position was reserved for me as a junior specialist, the section supervisor would not let me work. For two months I went regularly to human resources, and each time they told me there wasn't a position for me in the factory. I finally went to city hall and explained my ordeal to the human resources department head, who helped me get the job at the factory.

The same thing happened to my son, Volodya, and his wife Ella. After graduating from the Belarus Polytechnic Institute and receiving her diploma, Ella couldn't find work. As soon as she showed her passport to one particular place they told her, "Sorry, we have no openings." Her passport listed her nationality as "Jewish." Up to then they'd been prepared to give her a job.

Volodya and Ella Yakorevsky left the Soviet Union with their son on December 1, 1989, first to Vienna and then on to Tucson, Arizona. My husband, Solomon Isakovich Yakorevsky, and I left our home in the Soviet Union to reside permanently in America on March 8, 1993. Our children invited us to come.

We owe thanks to our children that we have now lived in the United States for 17 years. We bless this country and are thankful for it. America has become our homeland. We are American citizens and proud of that.

Rakhil Yakover

Ukraine

I was born in Odessa, Ukraine, located on the shores of the wonderful Black Sea.[1] I was the youngest of three daughters. The oldest was Esfir, and the middle daughter was Liza.

Our father, Sanya Abramovich Yakover, worked in an office and our mother, Dora Moiseyevna Yakover, was a housewife. She took care of the family, sewed for us girls, prepared meals, cleaned and did the laundry all by herself, right down to gluing together the broken over-boots that we wore over our shoes. Her life was not easy.

My father began working as a salesman in a children's clothing store in 1934. He was quite intelligent and clever, but he made many mistakes. Prior the revolution he was a salesman for a textiles store. After the revolution, when the NEP came into being, he and a friend built a sign that read "Yakover and K," thinking they'd start a business.[2] After NEP was abolished we were thrown out of our apartment. This was the winter of 1929, when I was a baby. My father was not allowed to live or work in the city, but only in the region, and my oldest sister was forced out of the Komsomol, expelled from school, and sent to a shoe factory to cut leather. She was just fourteen years old at the time; Liza was six. Our parents found a place in Chubayevka, where my father worked at Razdelnaya transfer station, two-to-three hours from Odessa on the train.

There were several years of famine in Ukraine. I remember my mother saying, "eat a big slice of radish and a small piece of bread," and though we didn't like it we had to survive. This was in 1933.

---

[1] Rakhil is the sister of another author in this series, Liza Iakover.
[2] The New Economic Policy (NEP) was Lenin's policy that allowed limited private ventures to move the Soviet economy in the 1920s.

Liza rode a tram to a school that was quite far away. When I was four years old I'd ask Liza to give me homework, and she would tell me the assignments. I would do them before she returned from school and she would check my work. By the time I was five I was reading, counting, and writing. Liza had learned many Russian and Ukrainian poems, which she practiced out loud, and I repeated what she said like a parrot until I'd memorized everything. I knew many poems on the school's syllabus.

We moved to Odessa after some time passed, and lived in a house not far from the city center, until the war began.

My mother had two sisters and two brothers, but by the time I was born one uncle was living in Palestine and another had died in Belgium. I don't know how he died. I know that he was sympathetic to the communists. My mother's oldest sister had five children and was busy with a family. By the war, the children were already adults. My mother's younger sister was a doctor. She was immediately drafted when the war began, and on June 23, 1941, she was transferred to the Belorussian front. The only letter we got from her came from the city of Borisov. The Germans occupied Odessa by October, and communication with Borisov was lost. My sister tried to find my mother's little sister during the war and after, even in the Boguruslan archives. The answer was always the same: "she's not listed among the living or the dead."

My father had three brothers. The youngest was killed by bandits during the civil war, and the middle brother, just married, went to Palestine and lived in Haifa. My father was the oldest of the boys, while another of his brothers lived and worked in Odessa and had two daughters. This uncle died at the front while my aunt and their daughters were evacuated to Azerbaijan. They returned to Odessa after the war.

My oldest sister got married before the war. Her husband served in the military in Moldova, on the border with Romania, and was immediately sent to the front. When they broadcast Molotov's announcement that the war had begun on June 22, 1941, my sister said she would go to the Voenkomat to be sent to the area where her husband was.[3] She became eligible for the draft, but when all of the chemists in

---

[3] Voenkomat is the military office that handled Red Army call-ups and enlistments.

the city were mobilized and sent to the Bacteriological Institute in Odessa, she went as well. They filled bottles with fuel (Molotov cocktails) to help at the front, which was approaching Odessa.

Her hands were burned in an accident there, and because of this they evacuated her out of Odessa. Luckily a kind-hearted classmate from her post-graduate school helped her when they left. She could not, in fact, use her hands. They evacuated on foot with the Pharmaceutical Institute, where she had graduated in 1938 and was then teaching. They departed for Nikolaev on June 30, 1941, walking because Odessa was cut off. People tried to get to ships and were attacking each other, but the ships would sail and the fascists would sink them. My sister made it to Uzbekistan. The last message we received from her came from Mariupol, on Crimea, but after that all communication with her ended. Her husband was in a hospital in Rostov-on-Don, though later she received notice that he'd been killed there. We still don't know what actually happened to him.

Liza and I went to different schools; hers was Ukrainian and mine was Russian. At the beginning of the war I had finished the fourth grade and Liza the tenth. Her graduation night was three days before the war began. Since she got excellent grades, she had just been accepted to attend the Industrial Institute. But the war changed that. And so began a different life.

On the evening of June 23, 1941, German airplanes bombed Odessa, but didn't return for a month. The bombing began around July 22. They'd often announce air raid warnings on the radio, and the sirens would blow. At first, people ran from their apartments to bomb shelters. Once everyone got used to it, they didn't pay as much attention. The children would gather shell fragments, rejoicing and comparing whose pieces were larger and hotter. There was an anti-aircraft gun on our neighbor's roof that deposited gun shells as well. There were two entrances to a basement where we stored various items and fuel near our building. When the steady bombardment began, people started going deeper into the basements. They'd found that the corridors were connected to catacombs on which Odessa stands.

At the end of July the fascist forces were closely approaching Odessa. They were stopped 20 kilometers away in Dalnik, where Odessan men mobilized and young untrained boys were dispatched. The boys from our neighborhood went there. None of them survived. I remember the bombardment began with artillery barrages, long-range shells that fell all over the city. At night we were afraid to sleep at home and gathered in the yard to watch for the enemy aircraft that rained down bombs. And so many incendiary bombs! Each neighborhood put together a schedule where people would go on the roofs to watch for incendiary bombs. And we watched for spies. This continued for 75 days, to mid-October. We still had to live, eat and sleep, and to wash our clothes as usual. My father continued working, and my mother would walk to the market. She had to cook our food. When anyone left the house the others waited tensely for their return. Very many people died in the bombings.

There was a garrison bath not far from our house where the soldiers washed up, including those from the front. The Germans tried to destroy the bath, but they destroyed all the buildings around it instead. Next to the bath stood a four-story house which was destroyed by one bomb. I remember that in the morning my father and I walked past that house, and from under the rubble we could hear a voice begging for help. What could we do? This was a terrible way for a twelve-year old to survive. It torments my conscience.

It continued this way up until the fascists began to break into the Crimea. Odessa was a major strategic point, a major sea port, so they needed to defend it with all available forces. It was the gateway to the Crimea. Fascist forces outflanked Odessa and made for the Crimea, while the Red Army retreated.

During the night on October 15, 1941, our airplanes dropped leaflets, which I will remember for the rest of my life: "Respected residents of Odessa. In view of the fact that enemy forces have surrounded the city and are making for the Crimea, and our food base has been taken, our forces must retreat temporarily from the city." They urged us to fight the enemy, to create partisan units, and to use the city's catacombs to make it easier. At the end was this postscript: "Odessa was and will be Soviet." It was one of the heaviest moments of my life. Several years later, in 1959, I was in the Soviet Army Museum where, in one of the halls dedicated for the defense and liberation of city-heroes, I found that leaflet. After 18 years, I stood and read it, crying.

172

I began a new life on October 16, 1941: a life of occupation, a life under oppression. There was anarchy in the city until 4 o'clock that day. Soviet forces were retreating, though the Germans had not yet entered. People plundered stores, taking sacks of food; horses ran through the city. The water was cut off. People searched for deserted wells or got into long lines for water. The first German units entered Odessa that evening.

To celebrate seizing the city, the German command held a banquet at the Soviet NKVD building.[1] During the festivities the building was blown up, apparently by partisans. In answer, the German command instituted true terror. Soldiers burst into apartments and seized everyone they could get their hands on, dragged them into the streets and hung them from trees. In Odessa there's a street called "Lieutenant Schmidt Street," which was once Aleksandrovskaya Street. This street runs through the city center from the train station to the sea at Peresip (an area of Odessa), where trees line the streets. People were hanging in every tree there. They hung 200 people for every dead officer, and 100 for every dead soldier. Near the cemetery, they built stanchions to hang people from.

The next day, orders were posted stating that all communists and Jews with families were to appear for registration and to bring basic necessities. On that day, people trudged in columns not knowing where they were being taken. There was a lot of down feathers from pillows in the city because the Germans thought nothing of ripping everything up.

Those who wound up in the first groups went absolutely straight into hell: to the village of Bogdanovka, where the men were ordered to dig ditches and to bury their wives and children alive, then were executed by firing squad. A man in our group had managed to get away from Bogdanovka. He told us what happened there and was blinded by tears from the horror he had gone through.

Our group ended up being taken to an Odessa prison. We saw the gallows on the way there. Closer to the prison, not far from the back entrance, we came upon a mound of dead bodies. Dogs were running around and on the mound. We were kept in the prison until November 6, 1941. The whole time we heard screams and shots fired, and in the

---

[1] NKVD was the Peoples Commissariat for Internal Affairs (forerunner to the KGB).

evenings soldiers would seek out young women. We would sit on the beds hiding my sister under the covers until everything subsided.

Of course, we had little to eat. We ate what we brought with us from home. When there was finally nothing left, my father talked to a guard (to whom he had given silver spoons as a bribe) and they let him go out the rear door. My father reached our home and took food, but our housing caretaker had brought in a Romanian soldier who threatened my father. My father told him: "Shoot me. I have two daughters and a wife in prison starving to death." Even the Romanian pitied my father and let him go.

We were released on November 6 (they claimed the Germans had taken Moscow and therefore we were freed). We made our way home but weren't allowed in our apartment, so we lived with two other families until January 1942, when all the Jews were rounded up in the area of Slobodka (an area of Odessa), where a ghetto was established. People lived where they could there: some in schools and dormitories, some in apartments with various other people. After some time they began to organize roundups to herd people together and take them by wagon to a train station. At the station they stuffed them into boxcars so full that people couldn't breathe, and took them 90 kilometers away to Berezovka station. From there, the trains went another 50 – 60 kilometers to the village of Domanevka.

The winter of 1941–1942 was very snowy and cold. During the day it would melt a little and would be wet underfoot, but by night everything froze. And still we were pushed further and further. All along the way we heard shots fired: they were shooting the elderly. Some dared to joke that there'd be a machine gun at the next turn to execute everyone.

We finally reached the cursed village of Domanevka. There were people who'd been forced to go there earlier living in rooms without windows or doors in a former school. Hunger, cold, dirt; Domanevka persecuted us constantly. But the most terrible thing was coming – a typhus epidemic. One after another, people died. As soon as a person died he was taken to what was called "the hill." There truly was such a "hill" farther from where we lived, where people died and were thrown into graves. My mother died from typhus, and my sister and I became sick with it.

After some time passed, when it became warmer, we were transferred to a different camp in the village of Akhmechetka. Conditions there were even worse: we lived in barracks on a former pig farm. The camp was enclosed by ditches and barbed wire. The camp was guarded by locals. There was no water nearby, so we would leave the camp in groups of 10, one of which oversaw the group. If someone tried to run away, or did run, they would shoot that person put in charge. For food they gave us one cup of corn kernels, or a cup of flour.

The Germans used the collective farms but needed workers, so they sent people from the farms to select people to work. Women were not allowed to bring their children with them, so at the beginning only single people were selected. Once the single people were all taken to work at the farms, they began using people with children. Young mothers hoped to return and take their children back with them. This didn't happen often, because the hungry children, with extended bellies and thin legs, didn't survive after their mothers left. The grown and the aged died as well. People worked from sunrise to sunset, all day in the sun, barefoot. Their main job was to weed the fields and gather ears of corn off the stalks. The workers were always overseen by local policemen.

I was around thirteen years old, and young people weren't sent into the fields. The teenagers worked in the huge garden at the collective farm, also from sunrise to sunset. We weeded the beds there, and when the cabbage ripened and turned we cleaned caterpillars from them. We were bent over all day, every day. It's true that we sometimes were able to get carrots, radishes, cucumbers, et cetera. I didn't eat cabbage for about ten years after that. An old man was in charge of the garden who treated us well. He would offer us watermelon when it was ripe, though we weren't allowed to take any home with us. We lived in a hut at the edge of a village and slept on beds of reeds. At night the mice ran around the hut, but it was better than the camp at Akhmechetka. We worked on the farm until late fall, and when the season was over we were sent back to the camp at Akhmechetka.

I don't remember how, but my sister and I managed to escape to the village of Koshtov, and persuaded local authorities to let us stay through the winter. We were prepared to take on any work, and to our surprise they let us stay. We did all sorts of work inside the barns and shucked corn. They planted hemp in the village, which we learned how to cut and soak in the river. When it was completely sun-dried, with the aid of a very simple tool we pushed out the center of the plant. We learned how to use a spindle. With the yarn we spun we made absolutely everything: shorts, shirts, bandanas, socks, slippers and other things we used in our home.

We were taken back to Akhmechetka in September 1943, and survived a fire there. It happened in the middle of winter, at night. We ran from the house, barefoot and naked on the ice. My sister wound up with huge, deep abscesses, and I had a festering boil on my neck. But we gradually felt that the situation was changing.

We weren't sure where the Red Army was until we saw troops moving, and by March we felt no one was interested in us anymore, and we slowly started heading toward Domanevka. Along the way, we passed Koshtov farm, where we had worked. We were tired and stopped there. At one end of the farm there was an elongated room dug into the ground where they'd once kept chickens. At night we heard cannon fire, and in the morning we spotted soldiers speaking Russian. We were surprised and scared. It all became clear when we left our cellar and realized they were Red Army soldiers. The Army was moving forward, pushing out the enemy, and we followed them. Odessa was liberated on April 10, 1944, and we returned to our home city on April 16, tired and hungry.

We went to our old building, where a very decent Russian woman took care of us. We called her Aunt Manya, and we were very grateful to her, not just for ourselves. When the Germans came to chase out the Jews, Aunt Manya wanted to save one little Jewish girl, Klara, who she loved very much. In turn, Klara also loved Aunt Manya. One day one of the neighbors said to Aunt Manya that if she kept the girl they'd tell on her, and the Germans would take both the girl and Aunt Manya. Klara and her entire family perished.

Our apartment was occupied by now, though we didn't think to try to claim it. We were told there was nothing left of our parents' furniture. When we were close to Odessa, six days before the city was liberated, we saw smoke and could smell something burning. It was a grain elevator. The Germans had dumped its contents into a huge mound, and mixed it with tobacco. They then doused it with gasoline and lit it on fire. But the locals shoveled up the steaming pile and mixed more grain into it, then baked bread with the grain. It was the first time we had eaten this sort of bread.

A woman who lived in our building was an orphanage director. She asked us to visit her, and offered me to go to live in the orphanage. I asked for my sister Liza's consent. I agreed because I knew that I would be well fed, clothed, and knew where I would sleep. I could go to school there. Liza agreed. We filled out the documents right there, and I left to live in the orphanage. My sister Liza found a job as a librarian at a naval school. After a little time passed, Liza was offered a one-bedroom apartment.

Ita Zeldovich

Belarus

I was born in Belarus in the town of Parichi, not far from Bobruisk, on July 29, 1920. My father was a farmer. Before the 1917 revolution my father and his brother leased three acres of land because Jews weren't allowed to own land. After the revolution, they owned the land. Each of them had six children. My older sister was born in 1912, and my baby brother was born in 1924. My mother tried very hard to ensure we all had a good education.

My father and uncle were forced to work on a collective farm in the 1930s. In those years it was very difficult to survive on a collective farm. We were blessed because we had our large house and garden already, and thanks to that garden we were able to survive.

My older sister married early, and another sister went to the Minsk Medical Institute. Because my parents couldn't help her financially she had to work while she went to school. She graduated from Medical Institute in 1939. While in school, she married a student and they worked out of the same home where my parents lived. By then, my father had returned from the collective farm.

My brother started at Minsk Medical Institute two years after my sister. He loved to write, so he worked for the institute's newspaper to make some money. As for me, when my father was still working I had to work on a collective farm, starting when I was eight years old. I was very envious of children who could go to Young Pioneer Camp, as we had to work during the summer.[1] We harvested tomatoes and tobacco, the so-called children's work, and had a quota that had to be met daily. We went to school in the winter.

After I graduated I also went to Minsk Medical Institute, so in my first

---

[1] The Young Pioneers was a Soviet youth organization for children aged 10–15.

year there my brother was in his third year and my sister in her fifth. My maiden name is Kitaychik, and when we were at school people would say, "there go the Chinese children."[2]

In 1941, when my brother was in his last year at the institute, the graduates told him they weren't allowed to go home, that they were all going straight into the army. It was said war was not inevitable, but we felt something terrible was coming. Everyone was saying the same thing: we will fight on enemy territory, and we will not give up one single piece of land to the enemy. So we were confident that we were in no danger!

It just so happened that my father came to visit us in Minsk two days before the war began. My parents wanted to visit my brother because he was going into the army after graduation. My sister in Parichi had a baby by then, and both of my parents couldn't leave her without help. They decided that my father would go first to see his son for a day or two, go home, and my mother would then visit. So it happened that, on the second day of my father's visit, the announcement was made that war had started.

People were immediately banned from leaving the city in order to keep everyone from rushing to the train stations. War was declared on June 22, 1941, and the bombings began right away, though for the first two days it wasn't so heavy.

At 11 o'clock on June 24, I went with my father and nephew (my older sister in Minsk lived with her husband and their seven-year old, who needed to go to school) to the center of the city. When we arrived I looked up and it was dark all around, as if birds had covered the sky. My father, nephew and I hid under an archway while the Germans bombed the city. The wounded were everywhere, and since we were so close to where my sister and brother-in-law worked that's where we went. They were worried and called home to find out if their house was still standing, and whether anything had happened. We walked, as the trams weren't running due to the rails being split. No one thought anything about us leaving.

We went home, but the bombing never stopped. The aircraft flew away and after two hours returned and bombed again. They flew low

---

[2] "Kitay" is Russian for China. Kitaychik, Ms. Zeldovich's maiden name, is a Russian word that can playfully be translated as "Chinese child."

and strafed people as they ran. They taunted us. My father said he couldn't do anything there, so he decided to walk home. I said to him, "Papa, I'll go with you. I have one more test in pharmacology. I'll hand it in this fall and continue my studies." We didn't realize what was coming. My sister asked us to take my nephew Mark with us, thinking the Germans wouldn't bomb where my parents lived. She and her husband would go to work the next day. At that time you weren't allowed to miss work, and even if you were five minutes late you could be put on trial. Back then it was very strict.

We wondered what we should take with us, which I remember like it happened just yesterday: we took bread, biscuits, water, and pulled a blanket from the bed to have something to sit on in the woods. Then we left. My sister told her husband they should walk with us to make sure we got out of the city and spend the night in the woods before returning.

We found out everyone was trying to leave Minsk and that no one should consider going to work the following day. There were many people traveling in cars and such. My brother-in-law said he wanted to go back to get a few things, since all we had were our papers. I had my passport because I could be stopped and asked who I was, and my Komsomol membership card because I had to carry it at all times.[3] I left everything else in the dormitory, including my grade book. We persuaded my brother-in-law not to go back, since we would find everything we needed at home (clothes and other things). I don't know what would have happened to us if he had gone back.

After three days walking we were almost at Bobruisk, 50 kilometers from our home. We sometimes carried my nephew on our shoulders, and because we had nothing else it was easy to do. When we arrived in Bobruisk everything was destroyed, so we figured the Germans were already in the city. We crossed the Berezina River in a small boat and aimlessly ran away from the explosions. We were certain the Germans were there and that we couldn't go home, so we went the other way. Sometimes at night we were invited to stay in people's homes. Several people wouldn't allow us in, because they were afraid that we would rob them. Several shouted at us: "There go the running Jews."

---

[3] The Komsol was the Soviet Union's youth division of the communist party.

I remember that we went to Bykhov and stayed the night. People there seemed calm and quiet, as if nothing was happening. My brother-in-law was in the reserves, and tried register at every military post along the way. He went to the post at Bykhov too, where they asked him to help with their payroll since his specialty was in finance. So he helped them. They also asked who he was with, and he told them about us. They couldn't let him in the army because they couldn't certify he'd graduated the institute, and he couldn't enlist because there wasn't time. They told him to take us out of the city, because the bridge over the Dnepr River was to be blown up in two hours and there wouldn't be any way to leave. Once again, we walked.

We reach Krichev Train Station in ten days, and couldn't walk anymore. There was space available on a train with open-air wagons, so we took it. A train finally left and took us to an evacuation center, where we were told we'd have to help with the harvest. Someone took us to a village, though I can't remember exactly where it was. It seems to me it was not far from Rostov-on-Don. We worked 10 days in the fields, morning to night, and received some bread and milk to live on. My sister found an organization and asked whether there was other work we could do. There was nothing, so we stayed.

Time passed and winter came, though we still had nothing. Our clothes were in tatters by then. A woman there looked at my sister's passport picture and wept because the photograph seemed like a completely different person (we had changed so much during those few weeks). The woman said nobody was going to detain us, and we could leave if we wanted. We decided to move on, and went to the regional center, where the trains were. With no money for tickets, we managed to sell my brother-in-law's watch and bought tickets to the nearest station. We rode on a mail train headed for Moscow with soldiers on board, who fed us.

We weren't able to get in touch with our family, and sent letters that in all probability never made it. We didn't know a thing regarding them. Our tickets were only good to Voronezh, so we got off there. Again, my brother-in-law went to the Army recruitment center, and again he wasn't allowed to go into the army. He was sent to work as a city auditor in Ostrogorsk, in the Voronezh region. They gave him money to move the entire family, so we all went to Ostrogorsk. By chance, we ran into a relative on the train who told us my brother had been killed on August 5, 1941, near Velikie Luki in the Kalinin region. He'd received his diploma and gone to Moscow with the other young men, where they were formed up as a medical team on a train. My father had thought my brother would survive because he was a doctor and wouldn't have to carry a rifle.

My passport showed I'd lived in the medical institute dormitory since 1938, and my Komsomol membership card proved I'd paid my dues as a student for three years. This proved I was a medical student. I was sent to work as a nurse in an orphanage for emotionally disabled children. At the orphanage I received shoes, underwear, and three meters of fabric so I could sew a dress, as my only dress was tattered. My sister and I sewed the dress by hand. She stayed home, and we bought some cloth and wool and made a large blanket for covers. People were selling things left by soldiers, which we bought at very low prices. We made socks from sweater sleeves to keep our feet warm.

We were in Ostrogorsk for about three months. Some of the workers at my brother-in-law's office had joined partisan units, which we wanted to do as well. But they told him he had to take his family away, so we went to the station to evacuate. We wanted to go to Tashkent, since it was warm there. A train arrived with boxcars to take us somewhere, but no one knew where it was going. Our family was large, so we needed a train with room enough for us all. When one arrived, we boarded.

There were Volga Germans on the train from Engels.[4] They were afraid to leave (and afraid they'd be asked to help the Germans), but had decided to evacuate. They were given only 24 hours to prepare for the trip. They had food, but we had nothing. I remember the train stopping somewhere on the steppe, but not at the stations.[5] There were sugar beets in the fields that hadn't been harvested, which we cooked and ate. I don't remember how long we were on the train.

We didn't know where the train was going, but it finally arrived in Karaganda, where we got off while the Volga Germans kept going. They

---

[4] Volga Germans were ethnic Germans living in the Volga River area who maintained their German culture. In WWII, the Soviets considered them potential collaborators and forced them eastward, where thousands were killed.
[5] The steppe is a vast region of temperate grasslands and savannas in Russia.

were being taken to Kazakhstan. My brother-in-law went to the military to prove he wasn't a deserter, who told him the same thing he'd been told every other time. He was sent to Balkhash, Kazakhstan to be an auditor, and they provided tickets for all of us. I believe there is a G-d, for without him we would have perished.

We met up in Balkhash and were given a room in a barracks. Someone came from my brother-in-law's workplace to check how we were doing, so we showed him the room. "Where are your things?" he asked, so we showed him our bundle made from the blanket. They brought in metal beds for each of us, mattresses, blankets, and everything else. We were very happy. My nephew didn't go to school because he had nothing to wear, and so he missed a lot. My father also stayed home. My sister found work and I worked as a nurse in a hospital not far away. In the winter I literally ran to work, as I didn't have warm clothing. The hospital was short of workers so I sometimes worked 24 or 36 hours straight. I worked there for approximately two years.

I saw an announcement in a newspaper that the Belarussian Medical Institute had begun operating again, but in Yaroslavl, Russia. I wrote and explained that I only had my passport and Komsomol membership card, but not my grade book, and could they possibly invite me to study. At that time, people couldn't go anywhere without an approved invitation. They wrote back and told me to wait for the invitation. I was working night shifts on the children's typhoid ward.

The institute's invitation arrived and I left. On the train, people were talking about how and where Jews were being killed. I had left my mother, sister, her husband and child, and my little brother, and I cried all the way. I had to transfer trains in Moscow, but felt like I had a fever. I decided not to go to a clinic thinking they'd have to quarantine me; I just had to get to Yaroslavl.

When I arrived they gave me a dormitory room. I took a shower with the door open, because I thought I might fall and lose consciousness. Back in my room I lay down, but I couldn't get back up. The next day a professor came and I told him I'd been in contact with typhoid patients, so I was put in a hospital for maybe a month or more. Once I was released I continued my studies.

By that time Belarus had been liberated, and the Soviet Army was in the Vitebsk region, where partisan units had previously been. They had an outbreak of typhus and were concerned the soldiers were contagious. Someone decided to send students from our institute to Belarus in the winter, after classes were over, to fight the typhus outbreak. They told me to stay behind since I'd been awfully sick not long before. But I didn't want to stay and went with the rest. We were in Moscow for two weeks, where we were vaccinated against all types of diseases and issued shirts, shoes, and socks before we left for Belarus.

Everything we saw along the way was so frightening: there were chimneys, but nothing else. The city of Nevil was completely destroyed and devoid of people. The only thing we saw on the streets there was a single cat, and nothing else.

We were taken to different villages, even though the Germans were all around. Another girl and I were in a village where the Germans were just three kilometers away. As we went from one village to another we came under artillery fire, and when we walked through the woods we could hear the bullets whistling all around. But we had to go, so we went. Only one girl from our group became sick. She recovered there and returned with us to Yaroslavl. We were in Belarus for around three or four weeks, then returned to Yaroslavl to continue our studies.

Prior to the war, during class, we didn't think about food, but now we were constantly hungry. I told my girlfriend that when the school year began we didn't eat just because there wasn't time. But we wanted to eat! In my fifth year at the institute I went to Balkhash to see my father and sister during summer holiday. I was persuaded to stay, to work at the hospital as a doctor because they didn't have enough medical personnel. They told me I could return to finish at the institute when the war ended, so I was in Balkhash on May 9, 1945, Victory Day. I returned to Minsk after that to finish medical school, which I did in 1946. Just before I graduated I married a disabled veteran, and we remained in Minsk, Belarus.

Later on, I found out what had happened to our relatives. After the war began, they'd loaded their things on a cart pulled by a horse and got about ten kilometers away when they were told the Germans had left. They went back to their home. But the Germans came back and took my mother, my sister's husband, their baby and others, and forced them to dig a pit. Then the Germans stood them at the edge of the pit and shot them. They forced my sister to work as a doctor, then killed her. My brother told us our sister's last words were: "Bastards. I treated you, and you are going to kill me." She was killed by the local police. We still don't know where she was buried. She was not quite thirty years old.

My other sister and her husband returned to Minsk after the war, but their house had been destroyed and there was nowhere to live. Friends in Kazan asked them to go there, so they left with my father. My husband and I stayed in Minsk, and another brother came to live with us to study.

People in the country were nervous, saying another war could begin. When my sister invited us to Kazan we moved there. My husband worked in a secret position in an optical-mechanical plant, so we weren't allowed to leave the country for several years. When we applied to emigrate, in 1979, both of us were immediately fired. Our request was denied until 1991, after the coup on 23 August. At that point we didn't know what would happen to us; we even thought we might be sent to Siberia. The coup didn't work, and we received an unexpected telephone call from the OVIR telling us to come and get our passports.[6] We got our tickets that same day, and arrived in America on September 11, 1991.

---

[6] OVIR is the office in the former Soviet Union that issued overseas visas. It still exists.

Maryasha Zlobinska

Ukraine

I was born Maryasha Wiseman on January 19, 1922, in Chernobyl, Ukraine. Our family lived there until 1924, when we moved to Kiev. My family consisted of my mother, who was a housewife, and my father, a factory director. His factory manufactured suede gloves, coats, and cloth covers. There were two children in the family: me and my little sister, who was born in 1927. I had 17 uncles and aunts and 19 cousins.

Except for my father, my family was very religious. My grandfather and grandmother celebrated every Jewish holiday. Our grandfather, who lived with us, prayed and celebrated all of the holidays in another room so that no one could see. My father was a communist party member so it wasn't safe for him to have a believer in the house, especially a Jew. But my father respected my grandfather. On holidays (such as Passover), there were separate dishes for my grandfather and no one brought bread to him in his prayer room.

Until the war I worked as a bookkeeper. I married in 1939, and on October 27, 1940, our daughter Esfir was born.[1] The first I heard of the war was when my father came home to tell us. He was born in 1888, and he was disabled during World War I. In 1941, when the war began, he was a deputy in the city council, and in the morning was called to communist headquarters and then to city hall. I was truly shocked. My husband, who was in the army and in western Ukraine training for two months, wound up in the war there.

Instead of evacuating, we waited for my husband to return, but he received orders to go the other way. We finally left, as the Germans had

---

[1] Ms. Zlobinska's daughter Esfir is also a Holocaust survivor.

occupied one area of the city already. My husband wrote letters telling us we should leave, because the Germans were like animals. There was no other way out. I left on foot with my mother, little sister and my tiny baby (Esfir was only ten months old) and with other retreating people and forces.

It was terrible to travel at night. We were hungry and not well-clothed. What could we have taken with us? We all went hungry. What would we feed the baby? I couldn't always get food for her. At night I would risk my life by knocking on peasants' doors. Some gave, and others showed up with sticks in their hands. Sometimes we picked things up that we found on the ground, but there was no way to heat water. We walked and were afraid of everyone and everything. My baby grew sick from cold and hunger. She had a very high fever and her little legs were paralyzed. But thank G-d we were able to get past the front.

On November 11, 1941, we made it to Novokhopersk, in the Voronezh region of Russia. We were barefoot, sick, and infested with lice. The locals there met us with open arms: they washed us, clothed us, and fed us. Before the war, all Komsomol members were required to learn a specialty just in case. I had completed a nursing course in the reserves, and in Novokhopersk I worked in an army hospital.

The war continued, and families with children in the Voronezh region were sent to the rear. We wound up in Akmolinsk, Kazakhstan. I worked in the Petrovsky plant there (manned by evacuees), where we made weapons for the war. I went to the military commission in Akmolinsk to ask them to search for my husband. In December 1942, I was called to the commission and was given his death notice. I requested to go to the front. My mother was still young and my sister was growing; I decided to leave my daughter with them.

That month, I entered the army and was sent to attend an accelerated course of study at a military school. From there, with the rank of a military medical assistant, I wound up at the front lines. I served in a mobile train unit: three passenger cars, a kitchen, living quarters for service personnel, and 22 freight cars. The train crew included a director (a military doctor), a deputy medical assistant (me), political officer, senior sergeant, five nurses, two cooks, and 22 nursing assistants. We picked up the wounded at the front and took them to a sorting area, and from there to an ambulance train. I was the only Jew in our group, which included Tatars, Uzbekis, Kazakhis, and Russians. Their attitude toward me was good; after all, I was a widow and I had a baby. The nursing assistants were family men, and they weren't young either.

I was demobilized in January 1946 after an order regarding women in the army with children up to five years old was issued. I went to Kiev, where my family had returned. I found them in a very frightful situation, as they were impoverished. Eleven men in our family had died while I was at the front, and five more were lying in Babi Yar.[2] Three of those were children. Three of us, two of my cousins and I, returned home from the war. All three of us were born in 1922. One of the cousins lived in Israel (he has since passed away), and the second lives in Chicago.

What does it mean for me to be Jewish? It means proving that I am a hard worker at all times, that I am dedicated. When I was a child, despite the fact my father was a member of the communist party, I endured such humiliation. I don't know if this was only in Kiev. At that time, Skrypnyk was Minister of Education.[3] There were German, Polish, Russian, Ukrainian and Jewish schools, and Skrypnyk ordered that everyone would be required to attend school based on nationality. If you wanted to switch to a different school you had to prove you didn't know the language in the first one. My cousin and I took examinations. I kept quiet while my cousin answered the questions. So my cousin went to a Jewish school, and I was transferred to a Ukrainian school. I wasn't allowed to attend the Russian school. At home we spoke Yiddish, though on the street I heard a mix of Russian and Ukrainian. We spoke Ukrainian in school.

After the war I worked as head nurse in a hospital. I married a second time, and my husband was transferred to Lvov, so I left with him. In Lvov I was a surgical nurse and a head nurse. I labored untiringly my entire life and took control of my work, because those years were difficult. In Lvov, I found out that there were followers of Bandera moving about,

---

[2] Babi Yar is a ravine in Kiev. It's the site of massacres carried out primarily against Jews. The most notorious of these occurred between 29-30 September, 1941, when almost 34,000 people were killed in a single operation.

[3] Mykola Skrypnyk was an early Ukrainian Bolshevik leader and proponent of Ukrainian independence.

and my husband – a member of the communist party – was often sent to nearby villages and towns to try to enlist people into buying bonds.[4] Followers of Bandera watched for people in the forests and would rob and kill them. I lived in Lvov for five-and-a-half years. We moved back to Kiev, where I worked for 28 years in medicine. I spent many of those years as a head nurse.

I have three children, and all of them live in America. My middle daughter left the Soviet Union in 1979, and the other two followed soon after. All of my children endured anti-Semitism in the Soviet Union, both at work and when they entered institutions of higher education. They were constantly hindered with column five in their passports, which required them to specify that they were Jewish. They all married Ukrainians, so the fifth column couldn't bother their children, but they still felt compelled to leave the Soviet Union.

It's very difficult thinking about the war. I buried many friends, saw the concentration camps and the burned cities. I saw the signs held up in Kiev such as "Kill the Jews!" and "Too bad so few were killed, we must get rid of them like bedbugs!"

What can I say about America? Thanks to America I am still alive.[5] The Jewish community takes very good care of us; they do all they can to make us feel comfortable.

---

[4] Stepan Bandera was a Ukrainian politician and a leader of Ukrainian national movement in Western Ukraine.
[5] Maryasha Zlobinska passed away on September 30, 2012.

About JFCS

Jewish Family and Children's Services of Southern Arizona's expert and compassionate staff have a long history of service. Since 1941, we have helped families in crisis, children and adults with challenges, people with disabilities, and elderly adults. Our clients come from all faiths, age groups and all economic backgrounds. JFCS offers a continuum of social and behavioral health programs that make a big difference for people during difficult times in their lives.

We appreciate the opportunity, through the JFCS Holocaust Survivor Program, to provide support for the victims of Nazi atrocities who live in Southern Arizona. It is the right thing to do, both for them and for those who were lost.

We are sincerely thankful for the Holocaust Survivor Program funders, which include:

The Conference on Jewish Material Claims against Germany
Jewish Community Foundation of Southern Arizona
Jewish Federation of Southern Arizona
Ellen Kaye and other individual donors

To contact JFCS:

Mail	4301 East Fifth Street, Tucson, AZ 85711
Phone	(520) 795-0300
Web	jfcstucson.org
Social	facebook.com/JFCS.Tucson

Our Partners

The Holocaust History Center at the Jewish History Museum

More than 250 Holocaust survivors from 18 nations have made Southern Arizona their home during the postwar era. The Holocaust History Center illuminates the history of Nazi persecution and its aftermath through the lives of those who were there. By sharing their life stories, these survivors have provided a unique body of information that allows something distant and ineffable to become personal and immediate.

Like the broader record of this history, the material at the Center is partial, haunted by absence. The impossibility of a comprehensive record vexes every effort to comprehend the past, and histories of genocide are distinctively shattered. Nevertheless, the search continues for more information about the lives of Holocaust survivors who lived for some time in Southern Arizona. Our intention is to evolve the record exhibited here on a continuous basis. The public is invited to join in this effort.

By placing survivors front and center, the Center takes a micro-historical approach to a presentation of the vast and complex history of the Holocaust. At the Center history is narrated by those who were its subjects not its victors. This is an exceptional approach to history in that survival was an exception in the Jewish experience of the so-called "Final Solution."

The individuals featured at the Center all experienced immeasurable loss. Many suffered mightily, and, miraculously, persevered to accomplish great things. Those who were there gaze at the past, they see us in the present, and they challenge us to do better.

Bryan Davis
Interim Executive Director
Jewish History Museum

The Message of Hope Fund
at the Jewish Community Foundation of Southern Arizona

The vision behind the Message of Hope Fund is a more tolerant world. This Fund was created in 1995 with proceeds from a very successful exhibit about Anne Frank that drew 65,000 visitors to Tucson to learn, volunteer and contribute to tolerance education. The exhibit raised enough money to cover its costs and to start the Message of Hope Fund, which began focused funding for tolerance programs on its 18th anniversary.

In 2015, this book project received a grant from the Message of Hope Fund at the Jewish Community Foundation of Southern Arizona to honor the personal stories and testimonies of the Holocaust survivors who came to Arizona, and to encourage intercultural dialogue in classrooms and the broader community on how to increase tolerance today.

The Jewish Community Foundation of Southern Arizona helps individuals and families, young and old, support the causes and organizations they care about, remember those they love, and give back in the ways that matter most to them. As a result, millions of dollars in charitable grants and distributions flow, year after year, into Southern Arizona, throughout the nation, and around the world.

At the Foundation, donors set up endowment funds to ensure that their values live on from one generation to the next, and the organizations and causes they care about are funded year after year.

Mail   3567 E. Sunrise Drive, Suite 143, Tucson, AZ 85718
Phone   (520) 577.0388
Web   https://jcftucson.org/
Social   facebook.com/jcftucson   twitter.com/JCFTucson